Jazz Son

Jazz Son

SELECTED POETRY, LYRICS, AND FICTION

Elliot F. Bratton

Library of Congress Number: 2003092128
ISBN: Softcover   1-4134-0327-1

This book was printed in the United States of America.

Xlibris Corporation
1-888-795-4274
www.Xlibris.com
Orders@Xlibris.com
18560

TO ALL JAZZ SONS & DAUGHTERS OF THE FUTURE:
PASS IT ON!

Contents

III

THE PROPHETIC ESSENCE

IV

WATERFALL OF TEARS, ECHOING LAUGHTER
(BLUES & HAIKU)

V

YOU BECOMING THE SONG BECOMING YOU (LYRICS)

VI

THE WIDER WORLD

INTRODUCTION

Why "Jazz Son"?

Before I was old enough to attend school, my mother bought me my first record—a recording by Louis Armstrong of "Hello Dolly". I can recall my mother's big smile as she took the little black 45 rpm disc out of its brown paper bag. I don't think I even knew who "Satchmo" was, but I know I fell in love with the song immediately. Thank you, Mom. Around that same time, my father, an amateur tenor saxophonist who had already exposed me to the sounds of Duke Ellington, Coleman Hawkins, Buck Clayton, and Ben Webster, noticed my budding interest in both the music and his reel-to-reel tape deck and recorded my first "mike break": a back announcement of Ellington and Hawkins playing "You Dirty Dog". Thank you, Dad. Years later, I would play all of these great artists' recordings on the radio as a DJ at WKCR-FM in New York City, and would even meet Buck Clayton. Despite listening to other kinds of music throughout childhood and adolescence, I discovered by early adulthood that it was this music we call Jazz which had worked its way into my mind's inner workings and taken my heart. I had done homework to the Miles Davis Quintet because it was good thinking music, and already understood what Ellington meant when he said "Music is my mistress." Jazz was and is part of my soul, as inextricably linked with who I am as are my heritage, faith, and basic personality. A "son of Jazz," then. Did my parents know? Or, as Sun Ra would say, was Fate just "in a pleasant mood"?

And what of the poetry?

Rhythm and words are inseparable for the poet, and I remember feeling inspired to compose my first poem by not only the diction of Edgar Allan Poe but also by the rhythm of a bus's motor as my mother, older brother, Noble (who introduced me to Poe), and I were taking the bus home one day when I was about eight years old. The task of writing this poem later involved both recalling the words that came to me and summoning the vibrations I felt on the bus. The possible link between the sounds of Jazz and the creation of poetry did not actually occur to me, however, until at least 10 years later. While I was attending Simon's Rock College of Bard in Great Barrington, Massachusetts, I recall listening one night to Charles Mingus's great "Mingus Ah Um" record and thinking, "I wish I could write poetry to music like this one day". From that seed, and the influence of writers whom, I would soon learn, had already written "Jazz poetry" and even poetic lyrics to already recorded Jazz songs, came the pursuit which led to my becoming a practicing "Jazzpoet" who wrote the works you now hold in your hands. I would be remiss if I didn't acknowledge those writers who influenced and inspired my early development on this course. First, Amiri Baraka, whether you agree with his politics or not you must admit he's the greatest living Jazzpoet today, and I was fortunate enough to hear him both with his "BluArk" band in a Jazz club and in a trio concert with saxophonist/pianist/Jazzpoet Archie Shepp and the late drummer Philly Joe Jones nearly 20 years ago. Langston Hughes and Kenneth Rexroth were two pioneers who, long ago, it seems, possessed an understanding of what Jazz poetry was all about and made the leap to practice it. Henry Dumas and Allen Ginsberg: the first a master of ancient rhythms, the second a wizard of modern ones, and both of these sadly departed poets were fearless originals and Jazz-influenced. Ntozake Shange and Sterling A. Brown for their respective abilities to profoundly evoke the flow of Jazz or its mother, the Blues, in their poetry just as a matter of course. Federico Garcia Lorca: he was one of the most musical poets, and he heard Jazz in Harlem before Kerouac. For their valuable encouragement: a true poet and teacher, Nico Suarez; Abiodun Oyewole of the most singular Last Poets; and the uncompromising singer/songwriter Ellen Christi, for telling me one day in 1985 that I should "improvise" in performance and, like a Jazz musician, take poetry out on that limb that any good Jazzpoet can.

In terms of writing lyrics, I must say that I'm thankful to God for the modest gift I have in this regard. The lyricist has a related but different gift than that claimed by the writer of poems. The key for the lyricist—no pun intended—is the ability to think in poetic and melodic terms simultaneously. I found this task a very difficult one at first, but gained confidence, oddly enough, from the example of musicians like Mingus, Sun Ra, and my late friend, William "Beaver" Harris, each of whom also wrote fine poetry and lyrics. I believe that when one is only the lyricist and not also the composer or collaborator with the composer of the music, you're on the right path when a kind of "channeling" occurs and the lyrics come to you through a process that feels something like acting as a medium—whether or not the composer is deceased—and you receive verbal messages from the music. Perhaps this is why so many of the best songwriting teams of Jazz and Pop (Waller & Razaf, Rodgers & Hammerstein, John & Taupin, Ashford & Simpson, etc.) have worked closely together for long periods and developed an almost telepathic bond. The only time I've been fortunate enough to even show my lyrics to the composer of an already-written song was when the recently departed Mal Waldron had been kind enough to read my lyrics to his poignant piece, "The Seagulls of Kristiansund," between sets one night at a Jazz club. Mal's encouragement meant a great deal to me, especially since he's one of my favorite pianists and composers. I also felt particularly fortunate when the legendary bassist, Dr. Art Davis, was one of the first to read my lyrics to John Coltrane's "Olé". Not only had Art made the original recording with Coltrane, but his approval of the lyrics was high praise indeed coming from the bass player who's probably played with more great singers (Sarah Vaughan, Lena Horne, Abbey Lincoln, Garland, Streisand, Eckstine, Belafonte, etc.) than any other bassist alive today.

The reasons for my inclusion of just one work of fiction in this volume, "The Wider World," are simple: it's the only work of fiction I've written thus far that features the music and its musicians, and it also "completes the picture" of my Jazz-inspired creative writing. I believe that I owe my desire to write this story and the more than a dozen other works of fiction I've written to my brother, Noble, who led the way by writing short stories when we were both in elementary school in the Bronx, sending me the clear message, "Yes, you can do this, too!" For my perseverance as a writer of fiction (poetry definitely comes easier to me), I am thankful to the great and underrated novelist John A. Williams, who responded to a question after a talk at Columbia University 20 years ago by saying: "If you're a writer, then there's no such thing as 'writer's block'." This gave me the confidence to trust my quixotic short-story muse, even when, as in the case of "The Wider World," this muse teased me with a story idea then left me for a decade before allowing me to complete what was started. I must also add one observation: it seems more than coincidental that at least five of the greatest writers of fiction of the 20th century were also Jazz devotees: James Baldwin (whom I met once in a New York

14

Jazz club), Jorge Luis Borges, Ralph Ellison, Toni Morrison, and Mr. Williams. Maybe this music's powers of inspiration are even greater than I have imagined.

Speaking of inspiration, I've noted in a line below the title whenever one of my poems was inspired by listening to recordings or to "live" performances. I'm happy to say that, after many listenings to "Mingus Ah Um" over the years, the poem, "Open Letter To Duke," finally arrived via the "vibration railway"—you'll find it in the first section, "Reflecting The Masters".

Keep The Faith,
E.F.B., 2/03

I

REFLECTING THE MASTERS

POEM FOR GIL EVANS

Veo el sol. "I see the Sun,

With the red flamingos flying all around him,

The Sun grows over the Canadian forests,

Rises over the black mirror of the Mississippi,

Rises over Mexico now, to meet Death.

Death, with his cool gallop,

Bouncing like pale Prez used to,

With a song under his black porkpie hat.

Now I hear Death sing the song,

In these last lavender minutes,

Death, I know your song is mine.

Come along, Death, come for me —

My soul is warm."

Go on Gil Evans, join Prez,

Bird, Jimi, Dannie Richmond, Mingus,

All the legends who truly live there,

Where flamingos fly,

Up from the skies, the stars,

Donde los flamencos vuelan,

Vuelan . . . .

"Bueno."

FOR BLACKWELL

(for Ed Blackwell from New Orleans)

At the edge of the crime there was a grin, rhythm, laughter,
Prophets in Jazz disposition, the applause flying in their ears,
(And money faded from their pockets), dropped dead on
    the way to the gig,
A pianist copped but wouldn't cop a plea, and a chair broke
    his hands,
Many brave souls lost years searching heroin seas for a
    saxophone,
While a ghost moans in every Jazz bar, after the last note's played,
Chilling the owners' wrists, closing devotees' mouths,
Buddy Bolden's ghost wanders and moans for deliverance.

But the children danced from the graveyard, marching to
    horn and drum,
With music so lively, they knew the parade done come,
Didn't that man with the clay-red face and African clothes,
Toss golden feathers as he whipped those tom-toms 'til they
    rose,
Rose like slaveboys, slavegirls with wished-for wings,

Rose like dancehall skirts and drinks when Ray Charles sings,
And in Morocco's mountains, where percussion fills the wind,
Birds fly in patterns inspired by the slap of hands on a drum
   skin.

Some nights ache for the release of spirit, for warm blue
   medicine,
A crowd collects where songs are born in darkly electric
   seconds,
Outlaw priests gather inside the hall, their purposes ancient,
Their skills crafted by a mouth-to-mouth tradition,
Their instruments steeped in a frightening brew of feelin',
They hear a far-off trumpet shout, no doubt it's Buddy
   Bolden's,
Witnesses start to tingle, nod, and hum, rin-rin,
Now swing the lights down, close the door, let the joy begin.

WHAT VOICE IS HIS?

(a poem about Miles Davis)

What Voice is his that's ever changing,
Becoming then undoing itself, swelling then weeping?
What Voice is his, restlessly ranging,
Like an oceanic spray of sparks to flames leaping?
What Voice . . . is . . . his?
Riddleofmiles.

Born with a Hamlet suit only he could wear,
Conjuring mud-covered ghosts or summoning cyborg sounds,
Always playing off of the screaming young cats,
Miles whispers in a voice so dislocated-hip-hypnotic,
Them 20-year-olds can't even dig him, not yet,
Not until they know the sound he came from.

He came up out of unadorned kings and undeclared saints,
King Louis Armstrong, King Diz, Saint Freddie Webster,
King Bird the Volcano, softly destroying himself,
Burning inside with a passive, monolithic exterior,
A cold mountain watching everything,

Darting eyes and a barely open mouth coughing,
Then singing the hottest, smoke-tinged lava song,
This Earth ever trembled in unison with,
Bird, the whistling mountain burning itself to bits,
Oozing lava laughter at some old clowns,
Juggling balls or needles, bottles or saxes,
Until the lava was gone and the empty mountain,
Bird, collapsed before the TV in Baroness Nica's flat,
Compulsion.

Can't forget King Clark of Terry and Saint Prez with his
    roundabout rap,
They all had a hand in grooming this cat of many voices,
Even before the record producers gripped young Miles 'til
    he SHOUT . . .
Tender sinews unraveled in the thin, dark air of his throat,
Leaving a sad teenager's voice,
Miles' alone.
Call him the rasper, frustrated yet creative, plaintive,
    selective,
Coolly mean, hot and lean,
Muted sheen on a blue-black dream,
He made the whole world watch and hear,
His horn, not his voice,
His songs, not his choices,
They all knew his tears but not his pain,
Saw his blood but not the opened vein.

Miles, the solar profile against a green haze,
Miles, high in the sky at fat time,
Miles, 'round midnight, saying "So what!" to great
    expectations,
Miles, some kind of blue cloud rising from a sorcerer's brew,
Miles, East St. Louis's country son wooing Nefertiti,
Miles, a prince of darkness who loved him madly,
Miles, a masked giant behind his horn, crying.

Miles and the press of the public, coming at him,
Like a storm of lights and thundering chatter,
He turns his back on them, but they can't stay away,
Like the recordmen he sacrificed his throat to,
So one day he would receive all he asked for by being silent,
Contradiction. Yeah, but Miles Ahead.
Miles s-s-smiles.

The man with the horn wrapped in layers of cool-burning
    bop and free-form funk,
Always thinkin' one thing but doin' another,
Underneath the Selim and the Sivad it's the same forward-
    looking master,
The old tribal seer with a host of young believers under his
    spell,
As he hustles a veneer of babe-runner, hip-drinker,
Drug-mixer, tempest-starter, vampire-pimp-on-the-loose,
Miss-stereomiles, mysteria of . . . mystery of . . . Miles.

Miles?
Oooh, the sadness moans in victory,
The house of stone rises again like an enchanted Spanish castle,
Inside, the trumpet blows, bluing, echoing, thrilling the guests,
With their black-and-white faces and distended, multicolor
    bodies,
Their fine clothes and a wasting disease mingling freely,
Then a microphone-stroking harlequin asks, "What sound,
    what voice is his?"
And Miles, the beloved decoy of weird brown star people,
Yes, the artist turns with that merciless heroin gleam in his
    eyes,
Lowers his horn, purses his lips, and whispers hard into the
    silence:
"My music is . . . what I say it . . . is. Dig?"

OPEN LETTER
TO DUKE

(A poem inspired by Charles Mingus's song of the same name)

Birdland's a jewel on the horizon,
A singing shore, don't you know,
With azure maidens proclaiming havens,
Lush embankments and fond embraces,
A gamble, a ramble, a wild whiling away of hours,
Where Bop poets sing of sweet, burning flowers.

You met Bird, heard his soaring word,
Steaming out of a white hot alto sax,
That summer night in Harlem's dancehall,
A red-dressed, long-legged, sweaty number,
Right before the riot started, she partied,
Apocalyptically franting, chanting, shaking, and quaking,
Promising unknown paradise and demise to all,
All who watched, bedeviled, as you were.

But you touched her, Duke, then took her home,
Kneading her body's passion-song until it became a muted call,
Afterwards you tapped a rhythm to the breathing of her
    sleeping bosom,
You watched from your bamboo throne, sighing, rolling up
    a white sleeve,
Letting black, brown, and beige fairies dance the mooche,
Sashaying, shimmying, and stripping along your forearm,
They left tracks in your warm, sandy skin,
Opened veins of romance, then sank in.

Duke, beyond our cheerful vamps and aggressive blues,
There's a romantic turn, a heart that wants and rues,
From time to time we even apply your colors to our flesh,
Before we exhibit new glories, casualties, to the paying guests,
And we leave them, always, with a souvenir of our
    impassioned quest,
Maybe a poem exploding with the odor of sweet, burnt
    flowers.

JAZZ ATLANTIS

What's been lost below our horizons of creation,
Our narrow routines, productive games, and frantic
　　assimilation?
Listen to the lower frequencies and you'll hear a civilization,
A democratic and harmonic, musical nation,
And rhythm is its business, promoting a melody of integration.

See the sax players, all young again and wailing,
Dolphy, Wardell, and Herschel, with Chu Berry and Joes
　　Farrell and Maini,
Marching in circles, keeping every listening soul in tune,
While Bessie and Dinah's blues outdo those mermaid and
　　siren songs,
Brownie and Booker Little swim a trumpet duet,
Blowing so furiously a sandstorm rises from the ocean floor,
Hey, there's the bar where you'll always find Lady Day,
She's sipping that ambrosia with Bix, who smiles a lot now,
So happy to see Bunny Berigan finally got started with his
　　one-and-only,

And they're whirling to Herbie Nichols and Bud Powell,
Trading bubble-burstin' riffs on moss-covered, white coral
  pianos,
Near Monk's shipwreck table, where he's writing tunes from
  his last seven years,
The basses of Blanton, La Faro, and Watkins start layin' down
  that ocean groove,
Pettiford plucks his cello, Charlie Christian grabs a guitar
  and begins to wail,
As Chick Webb and Willie Bobo float above it all, drummin'
  so heavy, swingin' so hard,
An octopus up and jitterbugs with eight lady seahorses at
  the same time!

Many more keep these undersea vibrations going,
Touching every sorrow with a joy, yes, each storm they pacify,
They can recharge eels, lull sharks to sleep, lift fallen spirits
  from the deep,
Legend has it that sea creatures called these musicians down
  before their time,
Because the greater, watery part of this planet truly loves
  the sublime.

A POEM FOR

RAHSAAN

You've been aboard my ship . . . beautiful ship.
— Rahsaan Roland Kirk

C'mon, take his soul,
Take him by the hand,
To that Promised Land,
C'mon, take his soul,
Take him by the hand,
To that Promised Land,
Land of Spirits, land of music dreams,
To that Heaven of Miracles he called Eulipia,
Take him from this plantation, Earth,
Let his blindness fall, let him see,
The indigo Sun that shines darkly,
And the incandescent orange Moon,
Take him from this Earth without peace,
Where nurses can blind little boys,
Where geniuses can be shunned as freaks,

Where maggots can have the power of men,
The power to make artists live in fear,
To stop a Black Jazz musician's recording with a White woman,
From reaching the heart of America because,
They want America to be a land of pain,
And you gave them all your soul, "for free" —
Now, Rahsaan, you can laugh your wise laugh,
Let them lie until they rot then die,
While you take your last voyage to Eulipia,
Through a sky of blackness filled with bright moments,
And when you arrive at the Gate of Sweet Mysteries,
Take out your three horns and sing a song,
And SEE the gates open to "Prelude Back Home,"
You'll walk to the place where the lion lays by the lamb,
There, you'll lay down your swords and your shields,
By the river of Ecclesiastes, rippling with waves of sound,
You'll board a ship, Rahsaan, one that sounds like a train,
And you'll get on board your beautiful ship,
Rahsaan, Rahsaan, Rahsaan.
Goodbye, Rahsaan.
Go on take his soul,
Take him by the hand,
In that Promised Land,
Go on take his soul,
Take him by the hand,
In the Promised Land,
In Eulipia . . . .

A FICKLE SONANCE

(Poem for Jackie McLean)

Ain't nothin' but a party,
U and the fellas blowin', sheddin',
Be-Bop/ High School/ Be-Bop/ Dance,
Be-Bop/ Smalls'/ Be-Bop/ Paradise,
With Bird, the preacher, the master,
Your idol with the sax, the hipness,
And the white horse/ Be-Bopped.

U, Jackie McLean, one of the youngest of the hippest,
Thrivin' on riffs so crazeology and
Takin' solos so scientific u must be
Dr. Klactoveesedstene hisself. No, u r
Dr. Jackle: creative and self-destructive altosax Ph.D.,
Blowing in the institutes of Davis, Blakey, and Mingus by
    night,
Begging for shelter at the feet of King Heroin by day.

Yeah, the King let u ride his foam-mouthed white horse,
Ride through your own home like a thief,
Ride on the bandstand (sometimes) like u had no respect
    for the music,
Ride into alleys, jails, smiling peacefully with your career on
    a line,
And u r up to your neck in heavy, quicksilver horse's blood.

But your ears could still hear a fickle sonance above
    quicksilver waves,
A song, changing, never-ending, fantastic,
But it kept fading out, then in, fading out when u felt the
    horse's
Quicksilver blood lapping against your ears,
Fading back in when u heard the echo of your wife's/
    children's voices,
And u struggled to be born like a baby with a man's brain,
Fought to emerge from a dead horse's womb, and
U busted the umbilical cord needle, vomited strange blood,
And cried, sweating, shivering, loving life as the fickle sonance
Returned for good.

MONK'S MOOD

(for Thelonious Monk)

That's the way I feel now,
So don't sabotage my music with lies.
That's the way I feel now,
And not the way of one second ago.

I always knew the diameter of the circle,
The sphere of sound emanating horizontally from my piano.
The instrument is pure, it don't give you no wrong notes;
Like Tatum said, the note's only wrong if you can't follow it up,
And any mistakes I made owed to a slight faltering of
    awareness,
Not a fault of the piano or my God-given and developed
    talent.

Some people thought I played just to hear my fingers sing,
Some stood behind my back and called me weird,
Said I couldn't play Blues 'cause they never heard me,
Said I had to record the same tunes 'cause they didn't want
    to hear me,

Said I was a dope fiend just so they couldn't hear me,
Said I was disagreeable 'cause they agreed they shouldn't
    hear me,
Yeah, they were sleepin' on me with their eyes and ears open,
While they made more money off of me than I made.

I only composed and played, trinkle tinkled,
The startling ugly beauty of brilliant corners,
'Round midnight, when the off minor keys whispered, "Ask
    me now,"
Or when I struggled to think of one terrible epistrophy,
With Kenny Clarke, for Brake's sake, but then Denzil Best,
He said, "Well, you needn't," and got me into a Bemsha swing,
Here, . . . a little rootie-tootie and rhythm-a-ning, there,
Some shuffle boil, before some criss-cross-lookin' critic,
Tells me he sees light blue spheres oozin' from green
    chimneys,
Every time I play, and it's real misterioso,
I said, look, here's a straight, no chaser,
It's for you, I mean you, Bye-ya!

Yeah, I always liked to see folks dance, move.
Music moved me like that all the time,
Down in my feet and to my head . . . until I got disgusted,
Stopped writing, then stopped playing, retired.
I resigned to the business, the rip-off, the misunderstanding,
But I couldn't, wouldn't put that frustration in my music.
Let's call this—"The Strange Rise and Stranger Fall of Monk's
    Dream".
No, call it—"Reflections of A Blue Monk". Nutty.

That's the way I feel now,
Don't distort my music with lies.
That's the way I feel now,
And not the way of one second from now.

ELLIOT F. BRATTON

THE PROPHET
DISAPPEARED

Poison in a glass of white fluid falling,
Burning into the throat of a Jazz promoter,
Be-bop swirling in his ears, smoke stinging his eyes,
Before him there's a hungry immigrant trumpeter,
With the Statue of Liberty grinning on his t-shirt,
Her Bible a checkbook, her candle a brass dildo,
The trumpeter screamed in a strange ecstasy, "My God!
It is Bird?!" "Nah, we buried Bird," a Mafioso laughed,
"It was somewhere in Vegas or Elvis's pelvis or a TV set."
"No, he's in my horn," declared a neophyte saxist, the latest,
Music industry pawn, mistaking a hundred-dollar bill for a
    reed,
"Eighty-six that line, kid," the club owner barked like Sinatra,
"Someday it'll be your day, but tonight's not your night,"
Just then a chance roll of the alcohol started a fight,
Between a down-and-outer who tied up his mind with heroin,
And a sweaty-lipped critic who had called Bird less than
    sublime,

Then Bird entered the club, with his hand stroking his chin,
His wings rigid, but flyin' high on angel dust and crack,
He whistled, "I'm just the invisible, echoing rub,
Who's returned for the horn I've been so long without,
I'll play sweet as a poisoned pussy willow, I'll knock you out,
I'll kill all you damn monkeys who dance on my back!"
No one heard the words of the Bird, but all felt a draft,
The yuppie moneytaker with a Cardin neckband opened
    the door,
At the club owner's request, and out went Bird,
Crying, realizing they hadn't heard his song again, as he had
    feared,
"You lying infidels, tomorrow's the time!" Bird said, then
    disappeared,
Without his horn, Bird, the Prophet, disappeared.

EGYPT EYES

(Poem for Nina Simone)

The high priestess came today, standing up on that stage,
Singing before the dark curtain, and overtones of guitar
and drums,
Her fingers pre-form words in the air, her voice follows
from beyond,
A warning surges forth from her full, triangled lips,
It spreads over us like a low roll of thunder before the clap,
We cling to this moment, to the stillness of light in her eyes,
All-seeing eyes, far-seeing eyes framed by Egyptian lines.

With a glance of those Egypt eyes, a turn, then a shrug,
Her guitarist and drummer pull the rhythm inside out,
The room moves, upsetting us, drawing us further in,
Her ageless throat beckons with calls, chants,
We feel the hum-strumming guitar's and shimmering
drumset's spell,
A song from as old as old but as new as now takes shape,

In this time and space, she sits at the piano, too beautiful
to desire,
Her Egypt eyes too terrible, too strong to be met by your
own,
Her *kuntu,* her style, shocks the soul like baptism,
Then cheers you like a little girl murmuring praise,
And you see the house of bougainvillea and red hibiscus
rising,
And she's flying in and out of its windows,
Brightening each room with high laughter then owning it
with Death's silence,
Like a mockingbird sings down the sunset before fading
into night.

JUST CALL HIM STUFF

(A poem to the memory of Hezekiah LeRoy Gordon "Stuff" Smith)

A virtuoso of the violin,
With a rounded chin,
And a worldly grin,
A long, gone Jazz magician,
Who conjured clarinets,
Turned strings into reeds, trumpets,
With a technique full of pizzazz, precision.
He wailed past segregation and Depression,
From coast-to-coast and then some,
Streets of Swing became his home,
Shared with the best in his profession.

Little Jazz, Ella, and Dizzy dug his violin's cry,
Fatha Hines, Sun Ra, and Nat the King bid him fly,
Is there any reason you shouldn't try,
To remember him by:

Flurries of eighth notes 'n' slurred tones,
Blues quotes 'n' buzzsaw moans,
Down-home grooves 'n' city harmony,
Kites of song flown in rhythm's sky.
Yes, the instrument's range he defied,
When he took the "A Train" by surprise:
A sound like his never dies!

You've heard enough,
Just call him Stuff.

TAYLORREALITY

(for the Cecil Taylor Unit of 12/12/84 at the Blue Note, NYC)

Dance, Brother, Dance!
Dance those fingers across a board of notes
And messages comin' at us so lightning
Hip/deep we cannot move from our seats,
Our eyes transfixed to our thoughts in sound.

Solemn, the land from whence we came on hearing
Of our spiritual return in gradual phases
Reaching from our bodies, we echo light and
Songs of past ignited by present deliver us
Into a/ Into a/ Into a/ Into a fleeing future
Running with Cecil's hands talking to each key,
Singing with white keys, dancing with black keys,
Praying silently into note after note of jagged bliss,
You kiss the inside of the hum of all blue men,
All true ends begin in the magic speech of your lipped limbs,
Striking and breathing chants through matter, urgently
Calling from brain-eye to muscles-fingers
Responding in the spiritual width of process,

The even speedier than e-equals-mc2 thought progress,
No one can make those sounds again, ever,
No one can reach these bounds like this never,
Cecil speaking in tongues dancing possessed with piano,
And possession never sounded so good:
Possession sounding like angels flapping wings,
Possession that's good for the soul in Cecil's hands,
Possession exorcising evil in controlled abandon,
Strokes of Cecil's fingers making wind move,
Wind move in leaps, dances, tap-dances on water
Only in Taylorreality.
In Taylorreality seeyourreality,
Hearyourreality in Taylorreality.

Reality like lines of air bursting with spectrum
Colors flying in helix formation 'round your sunlit head,
Music orbits through your waking dreamwalks,
Your living-smelling nightmare realities
Like the one Duke had of Cecil in the '60s sanctum,
Duke heard this sound familiar as his face but
Invisible and awful to imagine, yet pursue
He did, looking in dark moon mists of two azure swans' ecstasy,
Feeling the cold caress of a blanket of frogs,
Duke ran through memories of rednecked anger,
  whorehouse fears,
Took his overdressed band of warriors deep into the money
  jungle,
Turned some back so he could continue with Mingus, Max,
  and Trane,
Then went to sleep with his nightmare in the palm of his hand,
Woke to find his hand was quicksand, the stormy sky
Rolled with gigantic images speaking in tongues yet
Understandable, they said they were his brothers he never
  knew,
One had his blood and nerves, veins, guts on the outside of
  his body,

Another burned from head-to-toe except for two eyes of
    silver water,
Still another ran through the sky, a laughing, then weeping,
    shadow,
Another, a bronze filet of man, sighed with joy
As he drove diamond spears through his sides and watched
The fifth brother, who was but a sound measured by color,
Deep intensity green, tremolo wavering purple sound
    sculpting a man,
And distant as the drum music of the horizon of the Pacific,
There, yet there, moving, changing, living, Duke almost saw
It, it almost sang in his fingers, if he could've taken it,
And he could only, years later, call Cecil's pre-image "Brother,"
Close his eyes to this music and it lullabyed him as he died.
In Taylorrreality seearhythmorreality.
Rhythmorreality is Taylorreality,
Is yourreality Taylorreality?!

Find in your heart or a gutter's ugly reflection a unit,
Find this unit of sole, solid density with infinite space,
Find coagulated blood loosened by Moon to run tide-like,
Find the Cecil Taylor Unit standing on the Sun and singing
With helium flame light and incinerating the void to make
    light,
Jimmy Lyons stands with alto wand poised,
Crashing as distant galaxy's supernovas' instant suicide crash
Sits Andreas Martinez at the merciless throne of percussions
Steady as mountains dancing quickly through slow centuries
    to be lakes,
Bobbing, leaning buoyant, William Parker and his upright bass,
Honestly as shadows painting dark pictures of the Sun's vision,
Follows Frank Wright's preaching, crying, with tenor sax,
Wright the Reverend sings, bellows, raptures energy alternately
Flinging demons left and right with fists of brass,
Honking rude, shouting awesome, honking the good protrude,
Wright hurls venom'n'pearls at the bewildered thief-enemy,

Wright's winds scream in after-anger triumph-terror,
SCREAMS and calls Lyons in for the, THE
SCREAM! Can Lyons punctuate a *scream*,
Can his alto follow tenor in second-sight to . . .
SCREAM?! SCREAM, Lyons becomes high soul
Of screams, not starting but finishing the automatic heart
    transplant
From Wright to us to Lyons to us, now
Ominous beauty of honey heavy as lead spewing quickly
From Lyons' glowing alto reeling Wright tenor gladness
In horrible unknown happiness of rapture,
Hear the continual rhythmic screaming on and on,
Lyons leans stately purpose back, stops to behold
The storm roaring out of Frank Wright's horn,
The form soaring from out-of-style reborn,
Tempest sighs, rolling skies, leap from Wright's sax
As Jimmy Lyons' alto returns glowing white-hot

And sharp and suave Lyons pours lava through mowed lawns,
Gushes cool green fire up the backs of sleeping trees,
Igniting forests at an ever-quickening cobra's pace,
Fire, storm, rage to the kidnapping subtlety of William
    Parker's bass,
Parker tearing rhythms smoothly like rock quietly separating
Into faults, backbeat earthquake foundation swaying,
Playing in the abyss of time dancing reckless, surely,
At the bottom of the breathing flood of Andreas' drums,
Cymbal waves growing high, falling hard, echoing, chilling,
Drums rushing tones, bashing, swallowing bones,
Digesting spines in backs of those turning themselves on,
Yeah, the face of the recurring drum in forward motion
Leaves gasping silhouettes bouncing in the corner of the
    eye,
Watching Cecil as he shakes the multifaceted storm
    everywhichaway,
Fire sings around the hair limits of balding, unwanted men,

Storm screams a desperate meditation, charts penned in
    the abyss
Where bass rhythm's the only light surrounding a wild stream,
Cecil hypnotizes the liquid stream into solid alloy
Rising, climbing story-after-story, quicker-and-quickly,
A flood twirling from keyboard into the sky,
Whirling around and sideways without dropping a drop
Or a note of America's stormwatch without shelter
For the many, arms reaching to stop, but then
Transfigured into yellow fists of radiation,
For the multitude of lying-not-virgin ears who can't,
Can't believe they now hear peace emerging through layers
    of chaos,
Because all their lives are chaos masquerading as peace,
All their lives are chaos masquerading as peace.
Get hip to Taylorreality forreality.
For sake of morreality take Taylorreality.
Hear Taylorreality 'n' grasp yourreality.

Pressure seeks blood, voice seeks eardrum,
Mind searches reality's capillaries for hope,
The Cecil Taylor Unit chants known words in an unknown
    tongue,
The end is near, brother,
Swing without fear, hear dense honesty, cheer: Dance,
    Brother, Dance!
Danced those fingers across a board of song like only *he* can!

THE DENSITY
OF STARS

(for Duke, Monk, Randy & Sun Ra)

Talkin' about the strength of the masters, those tried by fire,
Who sat in Plato's all-night caves, teaching lessons of
flowing lines, circles of heat,
Lifting every bandstand with the zebras' dance and
elephants' stampede.

With no daytime, only the space to relax in orbit,
Night's bosom hums a memory, its lips drinking,
Its silent feet swaying and head bobbing, floating,
A smile ripples across the planets, joys concentric,
Shattering planes of sadness into sweet stardust,
Delaying comets on their clandestine rides home.

Below the burden of dreams, the moon sighs knowingly,
Above forms invertebrate, everlasting, dancing indigo
then white,

Seas roar and hush, clap and listen,
As whales moan, inspired by galactic singing,
There is much serenading, notes swimming their
chromatic leagues,
Before the lovemaking, gargantuan, droning, and ancient.

The masters chant together and levitate the initiated
without mirrors,
Sweat betrays an uncommon energy that burns inside yet
projects coolness,
As they play Shango's harmony of flashes of lightning,
Using the sacred equation for soulful music: the density of
stars.

STRONG SARAH VAUGHAN

Her deepest tones guiding us over dark waves of memory,

Then the Angolan falsetto rises achingly, high as the moon,

Climbing boldly to reach those forevers we left behind,

Making us wish for supposed-to-be's that never were.

Sarah, tempt us with beauty, then take us to a place,

Where perfection lives 'cause the Good Lord forgives
imperfect souls,

Thrill us with those rippling cascades of scat that you do,

Then bring it down with a soft benediction in blue,

Show us where we belong in your song,

Sail us away, past ills, hurt, and wrong,

Oh, Strong Sarah Vaughan, how could you have gone?

You, who showed us, like Sinatra, that we can't go 'way mad,

Taught us, like Ella and Louie, not to leave this place sad,

Because clowns make the festival, and clowns must be glad.

II

IMBUED WITH A MOOD

HEAR THEM PLAY
IN DARKNESS

(for Babatunde Olatunji)

Hear them play in darkness,
A music burning bright!

A vine of scarlet magic,
Grows from the deepest drum,
Tendrils greet you, start to dance,
Scarlet vine wants you to come.
A flute whispers sweetly,
Like a child, breathing your name,
A saxophone moans then hushes,
You step to the drumbeat of your name.

Sit inside the song circle,
Feel the center of the Earth,
Touch the brilliant ancient metals,
Kalimba keys to song's birth.

Believe in medicinal rhythms,
Waking your strength, chasing your fears,
Find your place in the darkness,
See the music with your ears.

The musicians wear their masks,
For they no longer have faces,
Spirits smile at you from their realm,
A melody heals you with its well-tuned graces.
Touch the ground with fingertips, soles of feet,
Dance the geometric lyric and rhythm of fire,
Return to who you want to be,
Be the light each theme desires,
Hear the music burning brighter,
Shake your soul, rise high and higher!

THE MIDNIGHT FIRE

Even when they called us slaves,
We had our manhood in our music,
We had dignity at the Midnight Fire.

Long past dark, way down in a clearing,
Us menfolk, we'd gather,
Our bodies weary and hearts sure,
With carved percussion, rattles, and fiddle,
We made a circle under the stars,
Made a lonely fire, then let it flow.

The rhythm rose with the flames,
And our voices grew together,
Then hushed, so the first story could come:
This singer had seen his children sold,
He ran to 'em, but an overseer's club stopped him,
He just watched his flame, yellow as lightning.

Next one boasted 'bout the sweet girl he missed,
How fine were her hips, tender her face,
He could still smell her breath, sweet as persimmon,
But Marse Henry called her to his awful bed and had his way,
She'd never be the same, black embers choking, snapping,
He stepped back, his face hard, shining like steel.

The last one caught the blue flame,
Worryin' his escape but dreading the lash,
He could kill them all but would rather run,
Find his place 'neath the North Star,
He'd go into the hollows, run down, down, below,
Alone with his freedom and the invisible things.

We had clapped softly behind our brothers,
Marking the beat for each solo,
Now everyone sang and raised it up,
"One more time," someone shouted before I poured the
    water,
So we raised it again, then hugged all around,
Bathed in smoke, hearts cleansed by the Midnight Fire.

LINES ON A SAXOPHONE

You can play these lines on a saxophone,

Or hum it, bring it, on a drum from Home:

West Africa, birthplace of our creative blood,

Before the storm, the harm, the slave flood.

A hypnotic line calls us from history,

To take these horns into a solo's mystery,

To make it new, from the heart of soul,

Just like the hip masters, the blasters of old,

Who put blues and spirituals into Swing and Bop,

With a drive from their times that wouldn't stop,

We've got to take R&B, Funk, and even Rap,

Let them function as guides to bridge the gap,

To the form we must create from the tip of the tongue,

The sole of the foot, and wind of the lung,

From a tradition as old as crimson memory,

Spreading the colorful seed of your community,

Four hundred years ago still lives in our spirit,

So make it dance, make it entrance a world that hears it.

You can play these lines on a saxophone,

Just-a-sittin' or standing in front of your home,

Just-a-sittin' like you was way back Home.

FUGITIVE FROM THE LOW‑WAYS

RUNNING
Jazz beating in his head: lonely, muted Miles,
Smothering the invisibly lapping river,
And the wish to forget a thief's handshake,
In the bar where dragons' smoke rose from chattering skulls,
As smooth and deadly as the valleys of the moon,
Shining down tonight, distant yet pitying.

RUNNING
Against maniacally severing daylight,
Populating Sunday sidewalks with shadows,
That startle loitering beercans, murderous alley cats, and
    old chocolate women,
In black mourning dress wrappers drifting weightlessly down
    the street,
While junkies gray as asphalt nod, buckle their knees, and freeze,
Beside tired whores in fake furs who groan at an unseen
    swarm of uplifted voices.

RUNNING
From cages of hatred, leashes of lies,
And crimes committed by those no one will ever catch,
He leaps over tangled barbed-wire bushes,
Soaring, past midnight, like his lost trumpet sound,
Then sliding, bulletproof, down muddy cliffsides,
And zig-zagging between battalions of navy-blue trees.

RUNNING
In the predawn, hooting jungle,
Waking pterodactyls, slimy caymen, and swollen lizards,
All slurping and crowing in the bog-land.

RUNNING
Happily sun-stabbed, over a blooming, olive and fuchsia hill—

RUNNING
Innocent again, down playful lemongrass slopes—

WALKING
Suited, but feeling naked, under the clear-sky sunshine,
Warm in the embrace of a gold-flowered savannah,
He raises his hand to his lips and the forgotten melodies
    return,
Shameless, now, he fingers the air, humming magnetic
    ballads to the God of All.

NEITHER IS JAZZ

Fusion confuses when it is called Jazz,
Like an artificial heart, it can't grow as hearts have,
Nor can it breed emotions in its plastic span,
For Jazz is heart and soul, not a mere muscle,
A fact some neoclassic jazzers have lost in their hustle,
Writing scores that slow the winds of change to a rustle.

When album and song titles become as opaque as
cellophane,
And the cover picture could be from ads for fast-food chains,
Then the cop-out has an audience and the sell-out reigns,
And there's music out-of-tune with joy, tones deaf to pain.

Societies tumble without a foundation of bliss,
So, too, will pretenders fall, without being missed,
Desperately, they wear the masks of friends, standing in
their footprints,
Hesitating, cause truth can't be a carbon copy, and Jazz
never is.

ELLIOT F. BRATTON

RHYMES FOR OUR TIMES

Black poets must speak!
All Black poets must speak!
To tell you the truth you seek.

Music is a spiritual thing,
What else can make matter sing?!

Harlem's the African-American capital, it's true,
If you ain't been in it, it still may be in you.

Black Man and Black Woman, different
Halves of the same wonderful, ant-covered fruit,
Growing on an American vine
With greedy, red-eyed ants growing from its root.

African-Americans ain't had no revolution,
And those without fear say it's the only solution.

NEAR≠YET≠FAR

(inspired by the music of Sun Ra)

We stand at the outer edge

Of the marketplace of classified souls,

Near-yet-far,

Trying to find

A common mind,

It's an age-old bind,

Like the discipline of ninety-nine.

We're here, we're there,

And

We're more than atmosphere

Standing on the verge of getting us on

The planet, yes, we must man it,

Instead of just looking in

From behind the veil of an open door.

We wait but, how long before we're in?

We be Humans but when will we

Be Beings in the Human Being?

Today, we yearn for the explanation of darkness,

The manisfestation of a world of light,

We move nearer-yet-farther,

We orbit in the discipline of ninety-nine.

HALF≠MAST

Faded green, worn black, and tired red
Are the colors of the drooping curtain
In the window of Smokey's Bar&Grill.

Fried pork 'n' peppers, a cacophony of familiar tongues,
Smooth carpet with an eerie too-red glow
That's brighter than blood, or
The red clay of the Sudan.
Brown men of different shades move with ginger ease,
Their booze-loosened lips arguing inconsequential events,
Far-flung schemes, away from the patient women
Whose waiting frowns won't be found here,
And it's so unlike the African fathers who once discussed
    their sons'
Strengths, the substantial affairs of the village,
And the regular economy of brown rice and yams.

There's a solo dance by a man in a turquoise shirt,
The juke throbs with Temptations, Taste of Honey,
The bartender stands with lowered eyes in a well-lit corner,
Glasses sweat in rugged, weakened hands.

In the back, a youth in a wrinkled lemon-lime shirt
Leans against the scarlet wall,
His pool stick at shoulder-arms, watching
The ways of Little Man, who slowly aims and
Applies a physics trick as old as the Pyramids
To move the cueball across the green until
It knocks the eightball down into the usual place.

Faded green, worn black, and tired red
Are the colors of the falling curtain
In the window of Smokey's Bar&Grill.

'ROUND MIDNIGHT CORNERS

(Inspired by the music of Thelonious Monk)

As I round your corner,

A bell says, midnight hour,

In each ear, a sour tear,

Look for you, but I'm too late,

And I circumambulate,

Watch each woman I pass,

Hoping the next will be the last,

Will be you, to explain my pain to,

"Don't you remember, the sun was shinin',

We were just mindin' each other, touching,"

Give back the time, I'd say the words to make you mine,

And you could complete the circle of my heart,

Tell me now, love gone, where you are,

And I'll leave this lonely boulevard,

Stop walking 'round these midnight corners,

Fading, as I'm waiting . . . for you.

A LUNAR DESIRE

I am the Moon and I am rising,
Attracted by the beauty your storms disguise, and
My breeze calls your name softly, softly,
I call to you, wanting you, sapphire sea.

I am the Moon dancing upwards,
Urging you to match my motion,
Now your waves rock back and forward,
I hear your heartbeat, beguiling ocean.

I am the Moon, and I'm gazing down,
Your veil of mist I penetrate,
You tempt me with cooing dolphin sounds,
How I yearn to fall to you, my Fate!

I am the Moon, and I'm running,
Chasing your tides from beach to beach,
What hypnosis is yours, what destiny's cunning,
Infatuates, yet keeps you forever out-of-reach?

THE BURNING MEN OF HARLEM

WE
We are burning men,
Burning through these canyons they call streets,
These uninhabited places that are windows on Hell,
We are burning, burning men,
We are like spitfire from the Sun, existing for reasons we
    know not,
But we burn, nonetheless, we move through life,
We're always burning for this, burning for that,
Burning for a real, a peaceful existence,
We burn for money, we burn for a fix, we burn for honey,
We burn for "Baby, will you give me the time of day today,
Will you not look the other way?"
"Brother, will you tell me the real deal,
Will you not give me some false opportunity to choke on?"
We are burning for real life,
But we're drowning in our own flames,
We are our own incandescent thoughts, burning,

White hot then black, until we glow with a blackness like
    the eclipse,
We glow with a blackness too terrible to look upon,
We are burning now, waiting for something to release us,
From this strange reality we call ourselves,
We are like a flame blown by winds it cannot fight,
We are moving backwards, moving backwards, backsliding
    through midair,
We are caught in a trap of burning men, burning,
We have before us now a dilemma:
We are up to our knees in lava,
We are bent, and we are melting,
What shall we do now, it's rising up to our hips,
We are burning like the lava consuming us,
The heat of frustrated thoughts and souls consuming us,
It breaks us like tree limbs caught in a hurricane of fire,
This heat is like the Rings of Saturn,
But this is not Outer Space, this is Earth, this is Harlem,
And lava is rolling up on us: lava of racism,
Lava of economic warfare,
Lava of self-hatred,
What shall we do now?
Put our heads in lava?!
What shall we do . . . ?
I beg you for a kiss!

THE CLOCKS STRIKE TWELVE

Hands clap in the dark of a theater's hollow,
Where few hear laughter and none will follow,
Breathless, I watch from the bottom of my seat,
The one-armed phantoms pounding the air for a treat,
While onstage, the living squirm: Oh, the hour draws close,
When I will eat and drink with the hungry host,
Betray me not, brethren, when the clocks strike twelve,
For, we know our mission altogether well,
Like a black cat waiting by the wheel of a hearse,
We lived and deceived in the shadow of the curse,
None will feel pain, nerves will choke on dread,
I will thirst no longer when clocks strike twelve, undead.

VEINS DRIPPING OIL

(for Cecil Taylor & Aime Cesaire)

Invocation of bodies twirling thoughtlessly,
In darkness of in-between sense and dream,
Where fireflies bend to bleed their lives,
In spiderwebs entwined solidly like a stream.

Begin the contour of body-to-body, and the tangent,
Confronts its angle and vomits where there is no skin,
A better world awaits the traveler, his eyes closed to the din,
A nearer light betrays yearning as her third eye closes in,
Perishing concerns, murdered tastes, smells drowned below,
A petal falls black from the orchid, vertiginous and screaming,
Its one care: the confusion of sheep; its one fear: the dark of
     the moon,
A boulder beneath each eyelid and underneath them, grass,
Water flows from hair to hair, fairies surf and crash on scalps,
Blood seeks its endless tail to eat, mercilessly, it doesn't know,
But there, there laughs an ancient of days, watching Eden
     die again.

A long while the skeletons have waited beside the killing pool,
Their eager jaws chatter in unison, loud like a Mardi Gras,
Disembodied skulls soon grow then shrink, beside the
    unwanted pool,
And pigs once eaten reconstruct themselves from cut fat
    and gristle pieces,
"War is over," the winner cries but the loser's spirit knows,
The loser's very blood knows there'll be another loser, and
    so they rise,
A skull and reconstructed carcass blistering the sunburned
    face of history,
Look at his arms made of sweaty slaves' backs and numbered
    paper,
His gangrened legs smell of centuries' pollution, how they
    walk backwards!
His sex organ has vanished behind a vacuum red as children's
    eyes at Hiroshima,
The stomach's walls leak radiation into intestinal tracts as
    noisy as subways,
Rush hour comes from the erupting heart, valves sizzling in
    misery,
Nerves protruding through chest cavity like bones through
    a tomb,
Help the veins, veins in confusion, veins carrying cro-magnon
    blood,
Blood filled with sharks with world leaders' faces,
Veins pouring hate in rivers swirling purposefully like the
    fingers of weavers.

What will the lovers awake to, how will they cleanse
    themselves of nightmare?
In the vaulted bathroom, water runs on their irresponsible hands,
They wonder if there's a price for every drop, a tax on each tear,
They cry, cry because their bodies have turned inside out,
And their veins are dripping oil.

III

THE PROPHETIC ESSENCE

SUPREME, AS NIGHT

(for Max Roach & Cecil Taylor)

A blur of angels, red angels flying from the lips of the fiery moon,
Enchants the night, caresses the night's hips, bathes in the
   glance of its stars,
While, below it all, rides the gang of winged missilemen,
Imitation angels of warhead mind and anger-fate demon
   design,
Missilemen of grayest-green-polluted-water color and stink,
Betrothed of the golden calf, sons of the sheep-sucking wolf,
   and without mother,
Theirs the mission of cutting blindfolds from the face of
   Justice and splitting her scales,
In the shadows of war, zombie drugs, and entropy of the
   mass consumption,
Of the dragon eating its tail in the circular chase of the
   blinding one,
The one whose house is a suicide maze decorated with the
   skulls of his servants,
Powerful men all, who lost their judgment and exited the
   maze only to find Death,

Now chasing the angels of the fire moon who must vanquish
 them,
These missilemen shall, in the last days, assault every tangible,
Although their destroyer is intangible,
Assault every audible threat, killing the meek,
Although their destroyer is inaudibly flying angel,
These missilemen will attempt to extinguish the red moon
 itself,
And whip the night until it bleeds white, nuclear flashes,
But all the human bombs cannot blow out the night,
"And neither can the missilemen survive until dawn,"
The prophets of Paradise agree with sharp delight,
For the angels of the fire moon have come to end the game,
To decapitate the missilemen, to open the doors,
Of a peace supreme, as night, on that day.

PRAYER FOR
THE SILENCE

(inspired by the music of Don Cherry & Ed Blackwell)

I pray one day I will be understood,

And speak to you without saying a word.

A restless heart is chanting in my chest,

Yearning for a land of human rest.

If I could leave this world without being dead,

Surely, I would be among all the friends.

Sometimes I hear a language divine and old,

That can be understood by every soul.

I pray one day all will hear it and learn,

And then the Voice of Silence will be heard.

TIME EQUATION

(for Sun Ra)

Time Equals:

The Essence be-tween Solid—

Fixed *concept*,

Clay-red brick set within

The black bosom of night—

A-nd Fluid,

Running *act*,

Creative reaching of 2

Hands for the Other,

So parallel

ELLIOT F. BRATTON

To the motion of Moon for Earth or

Earth for Sun,

The mid-point of 2 poles

Equals

(The Heart that never ceases to Beat)

The Equator belting the Earth —

(As Time supports Universe)

The Earth shapes the Equator

(So Universe molds Time) —

(To receive + transmit spiritblood =

Eternally living . . . .)

THE SHADOW OF HUMAN FATE

(inspired by music from Albert Ayler's "The Last Album")

The rapture of man's elegance suspends itself

In the chain of time, never to be regained by spirit.

The shadow of an ignorance cloud

Covers the path laid down by human hands.

The earliest element of experience

Lies in the memory of all time.

The time of human intelligence of

All is measured in an hourglass of Fate.

Until the human mind is like the axis of light,

Shining dimly through but brightly past the ignorance,

Humanity will never see its Fate and harness it,

And know the progress of infinity,

And know the way is good.

STARS SHINING

DARKLY

(inspired by the music of Sun Ra)

Universe is a star that shines darkly,
This universe is a star shining darkly.

Be unafraid of the blind void, always sucking,
Drinking your soul if only you let it,
You know this, so guard against this power of the pit,
Renounce it by being your true soul, seeing with true soul,
See with your third eye, eye of the universe.

This universe is a star that shines darkly,
Universes are stars shining darkly.

Penetrate the mind of All in you with your third eye,
The third eye is ever-vigilant, watching for you,
You must receive its messages to be true,
As your human eyes are physical windows to,
Your third eye, the invisible eye of truth.

This universe is a star that shines darkly,
Each universe is a star shining darkly.

Third eye sees by eternal light, needs neither day nor night,
Time revolves around this eye as Earth orbits Sun,
The Sun is the third eye of this universe,
The planets turn around it like lost souls,
Planets are windows to the Sun.

Every universe is a star that shines darkly,
Universes are stars shining darkly.

Before light there was the Invisible,
Known to all yet seemingly intangible,
The Invisible is mother and father of all things possible,
We, too, were born in the Invisible,
We, too, return to the Invisible.

This universe is a star that shines darkly,
Universes are stars shining darkly.

See with your third eye or see through Sun,
Each is given light by the Invisible One,
A light in darkness is this light, you know,
Like the dark light of the universe we know,
You see this light in the eyes of all you know.

A universe is a star that shines darkly,
Each universe is a star shining darkly.

The dark universe is not dark enough to blot out the Sun,
The universe shines with a dark light all its own,
This is another light of life we call "death,"
But this is the dark light that gave you breath,
Give up your "death" and then you will be One.

This universe is a star that shines darkly,
Each universe is a star shining darkly.

There are universes that no one's told you of,
Each shines darkly with this light of Love,
Holding stars of lightness in its hand,
Leading planets home like the souls of man,
Stars shine darkly in the Invisible's master plan.

This universe is a star that shines darkly,
All universes are stars shining darkly.

A MEDITATION
OF HOPE

A meditation of hope,
The song of faith shall begin,
The future's face still unknown,
Its voice chants in the wind.

A meditation of hope,
Our fate shines brighter than Sun.
We walk the infinite road,
Blessed spirits march as one.

We pass the Desert of Thought,
Guides have shown us the River.
We give thanks as we ought,
Joy will soon be delivered.

We walk through days without night,
Black universe is glowing.
We feel the wonder of flight,
Travel at the speed of knowing.

Hear mountains erupt with song,
As our souls dance in colors.
We see soul unity born,
Within the House of the Lord.
Hope in the House of the Lord,
Return to the House of the Lord.

ELLIOT F. BRATTON

THE ROAD OF
OBLIVION

(inspired by the music of Mal Waldron & Steve Lacy)

Tracing a man in greenest sands,
Stars mark my unlined hands,
As my sky-boat journeys past heaven and hell,
Treading the deep waters of time's well,
And I've forgotten what I was once,
Walking this road of oblivion.

Bathing in sensations mortals deny,
I hear demons laugh as angels cry,
Dancing, I am, in volcanoes' red layer on layer,
Then kneeling in the dew of dawn's sparkling prayer,
I wish I knew what I will become,
Walking this road of oblivion.

Spirit-warriors transfigure me,
Spirit-mothers soon deliver me,
Voices of saints engrave my brain,
Voices of sinners, wait, don't explain,
The erosion of innocence in all creation,
For, now I fly to meet my vibration,
The sea erupts, the time has come,
To leave the road of oblivion.

BLUE PSALM

Over me rests the bluest space,
Reflection of Your gaze, O God.

Standing in the endless, golden desert,
Entranced by the mystic traffic of the sky,
I saw Your clouds change shape like pieces of dreams,
And I knew not Your feelings as You created this vision,
I knew not the ecstasy and sorrow of the Painter of the
	Firmament,
Therefore, I am humble.

Touching the sands that live past every horizon,
I felt the grainy path of ancient thoughts,
I heard the call of the invisible family of winds,
Then came the roaring lion of the dunes,
His mane glowing white with the Sun,
O God, let me echo his windsong when my heart is full!

Smelling the salt of the ocean beyond the desert,
I stood before the dark blue stage of stars,
With the blood of the Earth in my nostrils,

I raised the ram's horn to my lips,
My soul sang the song of stars that shine darkly,
At home in this world, like the lion, I gave thanks.

Over me rests the bluest space,
Reflection of Your gaze, O God.

IV

WATERFALL OF TEARS,
ECHOING LAUGHTER
(BLUES & HAIKU)

SOME OLD MIRROR

(for Johnny Greenidge)

Some old mirror cracked, some mirror Blue,
An old mirror cracked, one mirror Blue,
Mirror cracked, like the Blue wrinkles in you.

You studied music, had gifts of words, 'n' paid your dues,
You studied music, gave gifts of words, paid them dues,
Dug Monk, heard Bird, were considered more than just a
crude Langston Hughes.

You said, "Ooh, baby, what she do that, ooh she, shake that
thing!"
Said, "Ooh, baby, what she do that, oochie woo that, shake
that thing!"
"I know I'm feeling like a singer reeling every time she
swings!"

Yes, his days were often short, and his nights long,
His days came up short, his nights went on and long,
And he could laugh in your face if you said it was wrong.

He got a little fame, knew some pain, worked for his
pleasure,
He got some fame, knew the pain, but worked for his
pleasure,
Lesser men thought him insane, thought he just wanted
to be a man of leisure.

One day his Blue mirror cracked, and his body fell down,
The day that Blue mirror cracked, his body fell down,
But he's up there smilin', even after he's in the ground.

So look in your old Blue mirror, please, and be dutiful,
Look straight into your mirror, please, be dutiful,
'Cause when you do, you'll hear him say, "Baby, you're
beautiful."

YOU GOT THE BLUES

You been payin' dues,
But they won't let you in the club,
You got . . . the Blues.

Bossman Blues, Salary Blues, Rent Blues, Money.
Sex Blues, Home Blues, Ain't-Got-No-Honey.
Blues like thunder 'n' lightning when it's sunny.

Blues in your pocket, Blues in your hair,
Blues in your mirror, in your underwear,
Blues is a killer too cold to care.

Blues like heroin, like a dog that wants your bones,
Drivin' you insane, chasin' you 'round your home,
No good to you at all, but can't leave you alone.

Blues ain't got no shame, thinks he's a lord,
Whippin' you when you can't pay what you can't afford,
Sellin' you downriver when you try to get your just reward.

They say when you got nothin', you got nothin' to lose,
But when you got somethin' 'n' it's nothin', too,
You got . . . the Blues.

CALL IT BLUES

After all, it ain't nothin' but bein' low,

Hungry, with no money, and no place to go,

A being so alone, and destined to die,

With no one to ask, 'cause who knows why?

Ain't nothin' but drinkin' until way past dawn,

Over a lover that won't go or another that's gone,

It's a feeling like night when no friend's around,

And all you can hear is silent sound,

You got to sing to it, baby, long and low,

Touch it like that love you want to know,

Kneel down in it, like hallowed ground,

Make someone hear you sing on the outskirts of town,

Maybe your lost will lead to their found,

'Cause what you feel ain't nothin' new,

Just sing and dance it in a circle, too,

Then smile at Fate in a pleasant mood,

Put that song right in your pocket and call it "Blues".

HEAR MY SHADOW

(for Andrew Hill and Langston Hughes)

Hear my shadow bangin' on the wall,
It busts through the ceiling,
Steps beside me in a cool shaft of light,
Waits, watches, a misterioso silhouette,
It adds time to my every move,
And sings the loneliest rhythm.

Hear my shadow flyin' over the beach,
Landin', makin' love to the sand,
Hear my shadow on the old tin roof,
Swaying to rainbeats and moanin' low,
Hear my shadow jump in ecstasy,
And watch the bedsheets blush,
Hear my shadow strollin' sorrowfully,
Pickin' up dust like a broken wheel,
Hear my shadow touching a mountain stream,
It melts away just like a frozen dream.

RHYTHM SPRING
(Haiku)

Wake up to me and
I awaken to you. Sky
Sings forgiveness now!

Smiles meet, yet stop, wait:
Hesitate. He melts, she turns
Green as Spring's wisdom.

Equinox changes
Us. We kiss at dusk, under
Old sun and new moon.

Blue clouds relent and
Spend their rain on couples who
Waited past thunder.

A new wheel of Love,
A drum song touches each thing,
Life in Rhythm Spring!

EARLY SUMMER NIGHTS *(Haiku)*

Hot Jazz, tenors roll
Passion, like ice, cools my soul,
Drums swing in control.

Train. Smoke, brother man.
That guy's piece is in his hand!
Search and Destroy plan.

All mayors know when
Urban fire riots begin,
Their old lies must end.

Memories of blue,
Black Blues distant as us two,
Baby I need you.

Hollow summer street,
Night's clear throat of sex sounds, sleep.
Listen: my bed weeps.

MOVE THE BLOOD
(Haiku)

Afternoon I slept,
Mind still rings with tones, colors
Like November leaves.

Last night the club glowed,
The third ear grew in foreheads,
Drinks fell, lost to Jazz.

Swing your head, tap feet,
Dance in seats to the street beat,
Rhythms spread so sweet.

Locomotive brass,
Rolling song on drums laid down
Independent, strong

Like silver tracks for
A train that ain't never got
To come back, roll on!

Roll, silver brass sax,
Pump silver pearls in black wax,
Send us foward, HOME!

Jazzmen spiral sound
Throughout a smoky room, BLOW,
Let Spring live in Fall.

So much to hear now,
Feel Bird-like, hungry for new
Horizons of flight.

But even men who
Never sleep measure their days
By Sun, Moon, and Dream.

Afternoon, and I
Must dream, because 'twas a nice
Night to move the blood.

WINTER GET AWAY
(Haiku)

Cloaked in brandy, he
Felt no wrong, played to be warm,
In love with a song.

Dexter held his horn,
Offering a pieta:
"You ate me alive."

Crosses burn for this
Music, hanging by its soul
Over the abyss.

Black men in disguise
Jump up nude and wail, without
Alibis . . . for you.

Don't care if it's cold
As a record company's
Heart, you got to *play.*

Winter can slap you
Upside your head, rob you, then
Drink your eyes with wind.

Would'n'you like a
Sax of white sand soloing
Over blue drum waves?

IF GHOSTS COULD TOUCH *(Haiku)*

And if ghosts could touch,
We would all be eternal:
Soul vessels of Light.

Waves of crystal warmth
Shine from her darkest eyes, now
A marimba plays.

What mountains compare
To the golden reaches of
Her legs, when I climb?

Her voice touches me,
A cool stream caressing this
Rock under the heat.

Dancers become song,
Naked union in Jazz time,
Love hides in these crowds.

Spin, my Destiny,
The mystery of your limbs
Makes me shout inside.

Touches captivate,
But yours will free me if I
Only surrender.

V

YOU BECOMING THE SONG BECOMING YOU *(LYRICS)*

ASK ME NOW

(Lyrics by Elliot F. Bratton; music by Thelonious Monk)

Don't you hear my heartbeat,
Calling down a dark street,
Begging you to come to me?
Won't you take my hand, now?
It's you I can't be without,
Don't you know we're meant to be?

My heart is just a dancer,
That's found a song to answer,
Won't you play my song for me?
If I follow its rhythm,
You could destroy this prison,
And free me with love's melody.

Bridge Chorus:
I've wanted you for oh, so long,
Wondering if this urge is wrong,
If I touch you and hold you near,
Would it be a mistake?
Am I inviting heartbreak?

My soul burns from waiting,
Fevered anticipating,
Wishing I could read your mind,
Like the moon before an eclipse,
I can't resist your sweet lips,
I need your world joined with mine.

Bridge Chorus:
I've wanted you for oh, so long,
Wondering if this urge is wrong,
If I touch you and hold you near,
Would it be a mistake?
Am I inviting heartbreak?

I would never hurt you,
Lie to or desert you,
It's you I can't be without.
I must be your true love,
Don't let our hearts be made fools of,
Come on, honey, ask me now.

CAN'T WAIT
TO BE NEAR YOU

Maybe detectives can wait for mysteries,
Maybe the prisoner can wait to be free,
Maybe flowers wait for the honeybee,
But I can't wait to be near you.

The insomniacs wait for daylight,
And a werewolf can wait for moonlight,
Even a madman can wait for insight,
But I can't wait to be near you.

Interlude.
Fate plays on its drum,
Can't you feel it hum?
A heartbeat unknown,
Is calling you home,
Come to me today,
There's no other way,
You're here, so stay.

119

Maybe the rose can wait for Spring,
And a bluebird can wait to sing,
The wise man waits for ev'rything,
But I can't wait to be near you.

THE HOPE IN YOU

Refrain:
Bring back the hope in you,

Won't you bring back,

The hope in you?

Daylight singing its song,

Its song is true,

It sings for you!

The world open its arms,

The world is new,

The world is you!

Get up, hold your head up,

See your path is clear,

Freedom is so near!

Refrain:
Bring back the hope in you,

Won't you bring back,

The hope in you?

HUMAN UNITY

Is there a child born hating all Blacks?
Chorus: No!

Is there a child born hating all Whites?
Chorus: No!

Is there a child born hating Asians?
Chorus: No!

Is there a child born hating one race?
Chorus: No!

Then, shall we adults hate any race?
Chorus: No!

Is there a child born needing money?
Chorus: No!

Is a child created by money?
Chorus: No!

Shall we adults need money just to live?
Chorus: No!

Shall we need money to be ourselves?
Chorus: No!

Is there a child born as a servant?
Chorus: No!

Is there a child born as a master?
Chorus: No!

Shall we adults have any servants?
Chorus: No!

Shall we adults have any masters?
Chorus: No!

Is there a child born that's not human?
Chorus: No!

Then, can we adults be unequal?
Chorus: No!

Will one child not help another one?
Chorus: No!

Then we must live to help each other,

We must learn to live all together,

Brothers and sisters sharing as one,

There's enough Earth for everyone,

Let the human family be one,

Not separated by racism,

Not separated by sexism,

Not separated by money greed,

Not separated by religion,

Not separated by false leaders,

Let the human family be real,

Let human unity now be real,

We are humans in death and in birth,

We are humans all over this Earth,

Let us now be one nation of Earth,

Let Human Unity rule this Earth,

Let Human Unity rule this Earth!

I'VE NEVER BEEN RESTED

I wake up to the screaming Sun,
And wonder where my dreams have gone,
I fight my battles every day,
But this war won't go away,
When will I find peace?
Will angels bring my release?
Today, I wanna be rested,
'Cause a body should be rested,
And I've never, never been rested.

The night comes, but not for me,
I climb mountains in my sleep,
I close my eyes, but not for long,
I hear the stars then watch the dawn,

I'm so alone below these skies,
Like lightning that never dies,
But my soul wants to be rested,
'Cause it's never, never been rested,
Don't you know I've never been rested?

How will it feel to be free?
Why does this pain follow me?
Why can't I stop this endless quest?
Come, love me, one who loves me best,
Take my hand, touch me silently,
Like the rain touches the trees,
And I don't care if it's just a dream,
'Cause it's the way I need to be,
Yes, I truly wanna be rested,
And my love, I've never been . . . rested.

JAZZ SINGER'S BLUES

There's a song I sing that only sleepers seem to hear,
There's a song I sing only the sleepers seem to hear,
It'll be around long after I'm dead, when people open
their ears.

I know all the clubowners don't want my song,
And I know those promoters don't want my song,
'Cause you don't need a drink for it to make your heart warm.

If I had a dollar for all the doors closed to Jazz,
If I had one dollar for every door closed to Jazz,
I'd have more money than the biggest record company has.

They call it a sin to feel high and sing nude,
They say it's a sin to be all high and singin' nude,
But how else can you float the beat or free the interlude?

When this dark age has passed, you'll hear Bird sing,
When this dark time has passed, old Bird gonna sing,
I can't wait for the wonders the new dawn will bring.

LADY, COME SING TO ME

Lady talking, fascinating,
I am falling and I'm waiting,
Be the lover I chase after,
Heat my hunger with your laughter,
The darkness always kills this dream,
And I awake with a silent scream.

Refrain:
Lady, come sing to me,
Pass your soul through-n-through me,
Blind me with your eyes' light,
Thrill me in your arms tonight.

It seems a wasted young life,
I need but don't want a wife,
I'd catch you if I tried,
But my hands want to die,
And my heart is just a whisper,
. . . know I want to kiss her.

Refrain:
Lady, come sing to me,
Pass your soul through-n-through me,
Blind me with your eyes' light,
Thrill me in your arms tonight.

Time, caress my throat,
Suck out a gentle note,
Lips that cannot think,
Touch her soft red drink,
Lady, bathe me in your taste,
Take me to the hidden place,
Take me to the hidden place.

OLÉ

(Lyrics by Elliot F. Bratton; music by John Coltrane)

Who can explain our lifelong devotion
To the ritual, *corrida de toros?*
What a fantasy, an unending dream,
In a circle of dangerous passions:

Feel the golden sword, birth-killing,
Stroke the bull's horn, loving-hating,
Aficionados singing,
O Allah, O Allah . . . Olé!

A small boy plays in a country sandlot,
The bullring becoming an obsession,
First blanket and stick, then cape and knife,
Now his wife cries at the blaring trumpets:

A widow's veil clenched in her fist,
In case this time is the first time,
The crowd will not rise to cheer him,
O Allah, O Allah . . . Olé!

Pageantry of picadors, proud horses,
For our fight with Death and her minions,
Will our matador be today's hero,
Or fall like the second one last Sunday?

The bull shook him, angry father,
Then the hooves stomped the green silk vest,
The crowd looked away, all praying,
O Allah, O Allah . . . Olé!

Our matador approaches the center,
The bull charges his first red challenge,
The cape swirls, the matador faces him,
A sword hides, the bull breathes, we are watching:

Our blood hot as the noon sand,
Thoughts pitiless as the white Sun,
Another pass and this crowd cheers,
O Allah, O Allah . . . Olé!

Our matador dances with the animal,
Bleeding him with the short blades,
His wife has seen this one too many times,
But not the black-haired woman behind her:

She drops her kerchief to the sand,
Matador sees it, bull charges,
And the crowd sings like a lover,
O Allah, O Allah . . . Olé!

Three silver blades and blood has marked him,
The cape rises and falls and he whispers,
The hooves kick, horns tear through the *paseo*,
Then the golden sword flashes to the heart:

The beast fails, quaking to the dust,
But the wife now knows her husband
Is a killer, she must run out,
While the woman with the black hair,
Smiles at the matador, who sees her,
Cuts off Death's ear, gives it to her,
The crowd cheers him, like the last time,
O Allah! O Allah! Olé!!

THE SEAGULLS OF KRISTIANSUND

(Lyrics by Elliot F. Bratton; music by Mal Waldron)

Time says I will never see you again,
No whisper of years can make these cries end,
I fear each time the storm comes,
I'll see your face as I did once,
And hear your voice in the waves calling my name.

Each night we would hold our lives in our hands,
Our limbs touched the stars then bathed in dark sand,
Before I left you alone,
And saw the slip of the Sun,
And heard the gulls like an alarm at Kristiansund.

Time says I will never see you again,
No whisper of years could make these cries end,
I know each time the storm comes,
Seagulls will cry in Kristiansund,
The seagulls of Kristiansund cry out my name!

THE SINGLE PETAL

OF A ROSE

*(Lyrics by Elliot F. Bratton; music by Duke Ellington & Billy
Strayhorn)*

I see your face near,
A single petal of a rose,
Your body shivers,
The flower quivers as it grows,
I touch your beauty,
Beauty only my heart knows.
Lightning wakes you,
You turn . . . to me.

I yearn to love you,
I yearn to love you in the rain.
Speak, my flower,
Tell me if you feel the same.

Your eyes say yes,
Your eyes say yes from your heart.
And I embrace you,
Love, stay . . . with me.

Bridge Chorus:
Like the warm rain,
Pouring wild and free,
Can our love be released?
Will you be my love,
Love me always,
Always, until times cease?

I touch your hair,
Rain falls on roses in the dark,
A flower opens,
Your lips tremble and part,
Words you cannot find,
Pull tears of joy from my heart.
My tears run to you,
Your hands . . . hold me.

Bridge Chorus:
Like the warm rain,
Pouring wild and free,
Can our love be released?
Will you be my love,
Love me always,
Always, until times cease?

I yearn to love you,
I yearn to love you in the rain.
Speak, my flower,
Tell me if you feel the same.
Your eyes say yes,
Your eyes say yes from your heart.
And I embrace you,
Love, stay . . . with me.
Love, stay . . . with me.

THERE IS A TIME FOR TRUTH

There is a time for Truth,
There's a time to remove polite disguise,
There is a time for proof,
When you must overthrow the rule of lies.

Refrain:
And when this time comes,
And you feel like freedom,
Then get together . . . get everybody together,
And RISE!!

There is a time to right wrongs,
To demand a change in your life,
There is a time to be strong,
To raise your head, look evil in the eyes.

There's a time for the just to prevail,
A time to seize Destiny's plan,
There's a time to help those who would fail,
To make history with your heart and hands.

Refrain:
And when this time comes,
And you feel like freedom,
Then get together . . . get everybody together,
And RISE!!

TIME UNDONE

Refrain:
Time undone, is it time that we're doing?
Walk or run, don't know why we're not moving,
So much fun, it's a crime that we're losing.

Does love steal time, or just slow it down?
We lived so fast, awake in a dream,
A tender train crash, a touch then a scream,
A king imprisoned, a queen crushed by her crown,
Crushed by her crown.

You needed me so, I can't tell why,
Eager to please, I entered your prison,
We threw away the key, a hasty decision,
And then I loved you, but why did you cry,
Why did you cry?

You carried a torch and carried it well,
I wore the armor, your personal knight,
But you burned yourself and I couldn't make it right,
Even inside of you, I still couldn't tell,
Still couldn't tell.

Refrain:
Time undone, is it time that we're doing?
Walk or run, don't know why we're not moving,
So much fun, it's a crime that we're losing.

Now, if you see me, don't say a thing,
There'd be that liar in your voice,
Denying the pain in our choice,
Playing deaf to a time bomb that's ticking,
Time bomb's ticking.

Refrain:
Time undone, is it time that we're doing?
Walk or run, don't know why we're not moving,
So much fun, it's a crime that we're losing.

TRANQUILITY

(Lyrics by Elliot F. Bratton; music by Bobby Hutcherson)

Take my hand that I might know,
Know your love, before I go,
There's nowhere else that I,
Can be, be me,
Be free, free . . . .

I watch the clouds,
Floating over me and I wonder,
Why must they travel endlessly over this Earth?
Like me, are they so frightened?
Or maybe they know what I don't know,
They know freedom, they have . . . tranquility?

Sweet comes the rain,
On a summer's day, all around me,
I walk between the raindrops, and am not touched,
When will I know the reason?
Am I lost, or have I discovered,
The magic, the glory, of tranquility?

143

ELLIOT F. BRATTON

I feel the fire,
Changing as it grows, but so lonely,
What I desire most in this life, before I die,
Is someone to share peace with,
Not just my love, but my freedom,
Freedom I found with you . . . tranquility!

Take my hand that I might know,
Know your love, before I go,
There's nowhere else that I,
Can be, be me,
Be free, free . . . .

2300 SKIDDOO

(Lyrics by Elliot F. Bratton; music by Herbie Nichols)

If I took a stance,
That turned into a dance,
And then took your hand,
For the sake of romance,
Would you dance with me,
Or fly away free,
As quick as you please —
2300 Skiddoo?

When you caught my eye,
Like a slow butterfly,
Then I knew that I,
Could commit a crime,
Just to have you near,
No reprisals to fear,
The coast's always clear,
2300 Skiddoo!

ELLIOT F. BRATTON

Bridge Chorus:
Baby, there are things this man can do,
To make my love a haven for you,
Don't you know that we'll never lose,
If it's me that you choose,
You know we cannot lose.

I'll walk Central Park,
Until long after dark,
'Cause you've made a mark,
In each space in my heart,
I'll fight lions, too,
I might even get bruised,
Just to be with you,
Let's 2300 Skiddoo!

VI

THE WIDER WORLD
(FICTION)

Clouds rode the back of the wind, changing shape and darkening with the storm's acceleration. Flashes of lightning bit the air, and the dark-muscled clouds slowly heaved roars of thunder. Streams of rain started to pour down the long windows of Lee Sanford's 41st floor cubicle. He stared in wonder at the scene unfurling over the Hudson River and what he could still see of the New Jersey skyline. Then he sat back down in his desk chair to read the entertainment pages of the newspaper. Unmarried, twenty-seven, and living alone, Lee felt unburdened by many of life's responsibilities. His position as a junior music editor at one of New York City's style magazines allowed him to live comfortably in an overpriced apartment on Manhattan's upper west side. His magazine affiliation also allowed him to attend nightclubs for free fairly often, usually to indulge his passion for Modern Jazz. This passion began with an early exposure to his parents' record collection which, like a pebble thrown into a pond, created ripples, ripples of interest and then of devotion, that only increased, radiating wider and wider, over the years. When he graduated from college, he had discovered that he already possessed a larger collection of Jazz recordings than his parents owned.

"Yo!" Lee shouted in surprise, his eyes fixed on an advertisement in the entertainment section. "The Hale Dodge Quartet at the And/Or, Tonight through Sunday," he read softly to himself. His mind drifted back to a sunny spring day almost 10 years ago.

He was in college, living in his parents' home in Brooklyn, and he had gotten the urge to study for his mid-term exams in nearby Prospect Park. Although the Brooklyn Public Library's main branch was close to home, the sheer brightness of the day impelled him to walk right by it, past the imposing Arch of Triumph in the nearby square, and onto a path that led into the Park. With a well-worn valise under one arm, Lee walked briskly until the whistling of birds replaced the droning of automobile traffic and he found himself in an open field. He climbed a favorite grassy hill, leaving behind him the West Indian governesses who pushed their employers' babies in strollers and the young women in running gear who jogged beside their dogs on the running path. Soon all he heard was the crunching of grass blades under his sneakers and the polyphony of birdsong coming from the trees on the crest of the hill.

As he approached the line of tall trees, his ears picked up a new sound. Mixed in with the singing and calling of birds was the sound of a wind instrument, a flute perhaps. Instead of immediately finding a place next to a tree to sit and read, as he had intended, Lee followed the sound. Taking long strides, his head jutting forward, Lee listened closely as the sound led him around the bend of trees to a place where the hill dropped off again to reveal another sloping, grassy field. There was a man sitting with his back to a tree and facing the field below, calmly playing a Far Eastern melody on a wooden flute. As he came closer, Lee was amazed to see that it was Hale Dodge—Lee's favorite musician!

A legendary figure from the "Free Jazz" movement of the 1960s who hasn't been seen in the United States in over a decade, and I discover him playing accompaniment to the birds in Prospect Park! Lee thought to himself as he stepped closer. "Sir?" Lee called, the seldom-used word jumping from his lips and the music stopping so quickly that he became even more nervous. "Ah, aren't you, ah, . . . Hale Dodge?"

Unperturbed, the musician lowered his flute and smiled. "Last time I checked, I was."

Emboldened by Hale's pleasant gaze, Lee walked over and sat down in the grass next to him. He regarded the older man, his skin a dark chestnut color slightly browner than Lee's own, and the black, curly hair on his head was sprinkled with gray and cut in a short afro style that led, unbroken, to sideburns and a beard of the same length and colors. Hale's deep brown eyes were intense yet his face was smooth and calm. He wore a goldenrod-colored shirt and black linen pants. "I dig your clothes, man, did you get them in Asia?"

"The shirt in India and the pants in Kashmir, my astute young friend."

"Wow! Hey . . . my name is Lee Sanford." He extended his hand and Hale shook it firmly but quickly.

"Have you been digging the sounds long, young Sanford?"

Lee nodded vigorously. "Yeah," he practically shouted then caught himself and added softly, "you're my favorite musician. I've bought as many of your records as I could find."

Hale grinned back, "Okay . . . . What are you studying?"

"Modern literature. I'm hoping to be a writer someday. But what brings you here? I mean, the Jazz magazines all said you were living in Asia or Africa?"

"Sometimes I am. Right now, I'm staying here in Brooklyn with friends. And I'm going to play a concert with my man Jaki Byard at Town Hall on Friday. You should try to make it."

"I heard about that concert but they didn't mention you in the papers."

"They will," Hale Dodge said as he slipped the wooden flute into a small canvas bag and rose to his feet. "I like to make surprise appearances, young Sanford. One's more appreciated that way."

As the slender musician made his way down the steep hill of the adjoining field, he turned his body at an angle for an easier, sideways descent. Lee rose and called out, "I'll be there Friday!"

"I know," Hale called back to him, one hand waving goodbye over his head. "Good luck with your studying . . . I left a warm place for you." With that suggestion, Lee scrambled back to the spot where Hale had been seated and leaned back against the same tree.

"Lee Sanford! What are you staring into space for? Isn't this your lunch hour?" The voice belonged to Wendy, who was arguably the prettiest—and loudest—junior editor in the office.

Lee snapped his head around to see her curvaceous figure standing behind him. "I was reading the papers and found this ad. My favorite musician, Hale Dodge, is playing at a club down in Greenwich Village tonight!"

"You and that Jazz," Wendy said, and began to file her fingernails.

"Hey, Wendy, I'm gonna go tonight. Why don't you join me?"

Wendy answered Lee's hasty attempt at a winning smile with a smirk of her bright red lips and a raised eyebrow.

"I guess that's a 'No'?"

"Told you last time, Lee, I'm dating someone. But why don't you put that paper away so we can go to the cafeteria together?" Wendy smiled, shoved her nail file into her purse and turned quickly on her high heels. As she exited the cubicle, Lee shook his head and grinned to himself. Then he watched Wendy's shapely figure ahead of him, her bracelets jingling in time with her rocking hips as she moved down the hall.

The rest of the afternoon, Lee's steps were quicker and his mind more alert as he anticipated seeing Hale play again. When he got home, he made himself sandwiches for dinner, ate quickly, then changed his shirt. He couldn't stop himself from scat-singing to his mirror as he buttoned the shirt and chose a new jacket. He emerged from his apartment building on Amsterdam Avenue to see that the rain had finally stopped and an evening sun was brightening the early summer sky.

"What luck," he laughed, "I forgot my umbrella upstairs!" Lee practically ran the long block to Broadway to get the subway train that would take him to the And/Or.

As he came up the subway stairs in Greenwich Village, Lee could see the sign with the club's logo in yellow lights up ahead: an ampersand, a forward slash, and the word "Or". Once outside the club, he checked his watch, saw it read "Eight-ten," and realized he was 20 minutes early. He walked to the tinted side window to see if anyone had been seated at the bar yet. No one was at the bar but all the lights were on except for the stagelights, and all the tables and chairs had been arranged for the first set. The brightness of the room made the club's royal blue wallpaper speckled with starlike swirls of golden ampersands, slashes, and "Or's" seem garish compared to when the lights were dimmed for the show. He could see the bartender, doorman, and a few other people moving about that he couldn't quite identify. Lee decided to go to the front door and see if he could convince the doorman to let him in.

"Hey, the first set starts at Nine-thirty, the bar opens at Eight-thirty," snapped the large, graying doorman, who looked like a retired wrestler whom someone had just given an undersized black suit. Lee took a step forward anyway, and the doorman raised his right hand in front of his chest like a stop sign.

"I know, I know. You don't remember me. I'm the guy from the magazine?"

"I'm not paid to remember names. Who might you be?"

"Lee Sanford, and I came early so I could talk with Hale Dodge."

The doorman looked Lee up-and-down for a second, then scratched the rough fat on the side of his neck. "Wait here, buddy."

Lee watched the doorman turn on his heels and walk quietly to the bandstand in the rear. Stepping further inside the air-conditioned club, he saw that the people gathered beside the low-set bandstand were Hale Dodge, a waitress, and three middle-aged, African-American men in dark jackets that he guessed were the other members of the Quartet. Before long, the doorman returned with Hale in tow. Hale looked almost the same as Lee remembered from their encounter in Prospect Park, only this time his salt-and-pepper hair was a bit saltier and he wore a knee-length, salmon-colored tunic and dark red slacks. "Do you know this guy, Hale?" The doorman asked, rudely pointing a stubby index finger at Lee's neck.

"Yes, yes I do," he said, and shook Lee's hand so naturally one would think they'd last seen each other only days before.

"Then, please, have a seat at the bar," the doorman said to them in a more polite tone, extending a meaty hand toward the barstools. They took two seats at the bar as the doorman left them to resume his position at the wooden check-in stand near the entrance.

"Young Sanford, you look like you're shaving now," Hale grinned, breaking the ice.

"I am. And thanks for remembering me."

"Sure, I remember that day in Prospect Park," he said, waving to the bartender as he did so. "Have you begun your writing career?"

Lee winced inwardly, feeling the stab of the one thing he feared Hale would ask him. "Well, as a matter of —"

"What can I get you?" The t-shirted bartender interrupted them with a smile.

"A ginger ale," Hale answered.

"I'll have the same, thanks," Lee said. As the bartender moved away to get two glasses, Lee looked pensively at the worn wooden surface of the bar.

"Why the long face, man?"

"Well," Lee said, his fingers picking at grooves in the wood, "I'm working at a magazine but I haven't written anything about the music for publication yet. Just edited other people's stuff and contributed the odd 'special interest' piece. I've had some ideas for stories—including one about you—but all I've done is file them away for later."

"Then 'later' is right now, man! Let's do it!" Hale rapped the wood with his knuckles, and the younger man raised his head with a start. "Ask me some questions, and I'll lay some things on you that I ain't told nobody. But you've got to do something with it, now. I want to see it published!"

"All right," Lee said, and eagerly pulled a pen and a small pad out of his jacket pocket.

"I'm glad to see you're prepared," the musician smiled then nodded his thanks to the bartender as he arrived with the drinks .

"All on your tab?" The bartender asked.

"Yes, and tell the manager that my friend stays for the show as my guest."

"Oh, you don't have to —"

Hale raised his hand slightly and Lee stopped his mild protest. "Where were we, young Sanford?"

Lee studied Hale's face for a moment and took a short sip from his glass. His thoughts focused on questions rising, colliding, breaking apart then re-forming inside his mind. Hale waited, looking away from Lee but at nothing in particular.

"Did you ever meet—or even play with—John Coltrane?"

Hale Dodge grinned broadly, deliberately raised his right hand and brought it down with the index finger pointing at an indiscriminate spot on the bar counter. "*That's* the kind of question I'm talking about," he said at last. Then he stared into Lee's eyes solemnly. "Yes, I met Trane and we did play together a few times.

"I think it was late 1966, not that long before he died," Hale cleared his throat thoughtfully. "At the time, Trane was experimenting—it was all about sound and the spirit. So he was very open. He'd let people sit in and play as freely as they wanted to . . . especially the drummers and horn players. Pharoah Sanders—I knew him from my hometown, San Francisco—he introduced me to Trane, and soon after that we all played a few gigs together. That was something: John Coltrane, Pharoah, and myself, all playing tenor together!"

"So that was the group with Jimmy Garrison, Rashied Ali, and Alice Coltrane?"

"Right, but sometimes he had percussionists, too. And on the more meditative pieces, I played flute. You know, Trane was a man of few words but what he said counted. One thing he said to me was that he, that he—" Hale rubbed his forehead and frowned for a second. "He said he 'heard the messages' coming from my flute. And you know, he was the first person to ever talk to me like that."

"That must have been some encouragement, coming from him?!"

"Yes, such a compliment. But it also stopped me, froze my thinking for a second. You see, he'd just stepped onto another plane with that observation. I had to look at what I played all the time in a different way after that in terms of what I was communicating to others spiritually. I became very careful about sending the right messages out to particular people in particular places, and at particular times."

"Cool. Was it through Pharoah that you also met Don Cherry?"

"Oh, I see you've done your homework, young Sanford!" Hale raised his eyes to the ceiling and smiled. "Y'know, nobody asks me how I met Don but they all want to know what it was like playing folk tunes with him in Asia and Africa and such. Pharoah introduced us. Mainly, I thought, because he wanted to stick with Trane and he knew I could fit into Don's concept, Don's desire to explore other cultures and unite the music under his own umbrella. Don was like Ornette Coleman's main disciple but then, when he went out on his own, Don took the freedom thing his own way and blended it with folk forms from all over the world."

"I've got an import of you and Don at a festival in North Africa, I think?"

"It could be, I know they're out there. I think two recordings we got paid small money for, and one—I think it's that one from North Africa . . . Tangiers—we didn't even know they recorded it until years later."

"It's a bootleg recording?"

"Man, you know what Rahsaan Roland Kirk said: 'The business ain't nothin' but the blues'. And that's 'blues' with a small 'b,' man".

"And around 1969 you left Don's group to join Sun Ra and his Arkestra?"

"Yeah, Don and I parted 'cause he would be traveling on, and I wanted to get back to the States. So I found the Arkestra in Paris and sat in. I made it a point to only play bass clarinet and percussion. Why, John Gilmore was playing so much tenor, and all of Sunny's reedmen could play flute, so the bass clarinet was the only thing could make me stand out! Hearing me on bass clarinet, Sun Ra let me come back to the States with the Arkestra."

"Had you started playing soprano sax yet?" Lee asked, writing hurriedly in his notepad.

"No, but it was Sunny who convinced me to pick it up. I think he had a feeling I'd make a mark with it."

The owner of the And/Or, a short, slightly overweight man with his gray hair pulled tight into a long ponytail, appeared at the musician's elbow and whispered in his ear. Lee wrote something in his pad and, when he looked up, the club owner was gone.

"That means I gotta go," Hale said as he rose from his barstool. "But, dig. You've already got some things in that pad I never told any critic."

Sensing that he might not get another chance to ask him something that night, Lee also rose and called, "I've never seen you with your own group before. What should I listen for?"

The musician turned, cocked his head to the side, and peered at Lee. "Listen for those messages. The wider world is in this music, if you're open to it."

As Lee thought about Hale's answer, an odd feeling came over him, like all his expectations of that day had focused themselves into this one moment. The noise of the Jazz club was now a distant hum, and the movement of its people around him was like the anonymous passing of falling leaves or flying birds overhead. He scarcely noticed that the Quartet had now assembled on the bandstand, talking quietly among themselves as they readied their instruments and music stands. Even the dimming of the lights and the club owner's announcement of the Hale Dodge Quartet failed to break the spell. Without really being conscious of it, Lee's eyes focused on Hale holding his soprano saxophone against his side. "Thank you," Hale's voice cut through the polite applause. "I call this first piece 'Rings of Saturn'. Listen. Dig the sounds."

Hale brought the mouthpiece of the instrument to his lips, and a simple, Near Eastern-sounding melody poured slowly, a cappella, from the sax, its effect hypnotic as he repeated it again and again. Then the saxophone's passages were joined by an insistent pulse from the upright bass, and

a light but rapid tapping of the ride cymbal punctuated by
bass drum accents. The pianist added to the growing tension
with a series of North African modal runs, then the drummer
answered him with tom-tom beats. A cymbal crash ushered
in a change in melody as the soprano and the piano came
together, delivering a unison theme that seemed strange at
first but was really a variation on the first melody. Lee was
listening intently, his eyes transfixed to the bell of Hale's
golden horn. As Hale's solo began, Lee's gaze filled with the
darkness in the bell of the horn. This darkness became
magnified and the music seemed to amplify itself in his mind
until he felt surrounded by blackness and music, was
conscious only of blackness and music. The music pulled
him inward until he was aware of lights rushing steadily but
peacefully toward him, and then passing overhead and to
the side of him. When his eyes focused on the lights, he
could tell they were not man-made electric lights but natural
stars, stars burning as in outer space. His consciousness was
being advanced, pulled forward, forward to a destination
he could not yet see. A comet sailed silently by, arcing over
him and then away, to the left. Meteors hovered like bubbles
then rose, their rock-like forms disappearing over his head.
And then he saw the rings, the bright, icy bands spinning
noiselessly around Saturn.

Still hearing the music of the Quartet, Lee stared at the
rings and the planet suspended in their midst. Ice spray
from the rings swept over him like the mist of a waterfall. A
great wind howled in time with climaxes in the music, its
tone softening then rising again. As his consciousness was
enveloped in the swirling rush of the rings, the howling took
on a more distinct sound, and he recognized it to be a chorus
of voices echoing, pulse-like, from deep within the planet.
He moved, speeding within the rings, circling Saturn's yellow,
haze-colored mass, and the voices grew louder, louder until
he could hear a kind of solfeggio song. He listened, cycling
at an unfathomable speed, and the song was everywhere,

rising like the great wind from Saturn's surface. While he couldn't understand the language of the singing, Lee began to comprehend that the tones were the same as those coming from Hale's horn, flowing simultaneously as if sung by a harmonic multitude. And as Hale's playing grew louder, the multitude's volume rose also, swelling as his solo reached its peak.

When the multitude of voices trailed off, echoing a little with the soprano's last note, Lee's vision started to telescope backward, out of the rings, away from the distant planet. Scarlet, white, orange, and blue star clusters seemed to rise then fall beneath him rapidly, disappearing like a shower of sparks created by an unseen, celestial anvil. The stars spun away until there was only blackness. And then he saw the bell of the horn, dark, silent, and then swaying downward as Hale lowered the instrument to his side.

Lee heard the audience's applause and shook involuntarily, his right arm reaching out to the bar ledge for support and bumping into, almost knocking over, his glass of ginger ale. He grabbed the glass, steadied it, and turned, blinking around the dimly-lit club. He saw the audience and the faces of the band members, and felt oddly like he had been away from them for a long time. His mouth opened to speak but nothing came out. He looked at Hale's face and searched for his eyes, but saw they were closed while his body swayed back-and-forth to the music's slowly lilting, hypnotic rhythm. Hale seemed like a participant in a ritual, his body dancing, waiting for its next inspiration while his face wore the mask of his magic.

The pianist's and then the drummer's solos passed with Lee's mind still riding the wave of Hale's sound, feeling the effect of its vision. When the saxophonist re-entered after the drum solo and locked in with the pianist, they returned to the theme. Lee focused again on the bell of the horn. No stars, planetary rings or other cosmic bodies rose before him this time. But Lee did hear the wind, and then the harmonic multitude faintly echoing the melody to "Rings of Saturn". When the song ended, he clapped along with the crowd then ordered a fresh ginger ale. He wondered to himself, *What just happened? There were no hallucinogens in my ginger ale, were there?* The bartender set the new glass down and Lee raised it, the bubbles caressing the flesh under his nose. He drank, then smiled to himself. "I think you'll all know this one," Hale said, and lifted his tenor sax from its rest on the bandstand. Lee put his glass back on the bar and grabbed his notepad. Before the song started, he glanced about the room, taking in the atmosphere. He wrote:

> *As the audience members made their last friendly comments and witty asides to their neighbors, the saxophonist blew into his instrument. He began playing, unaccompanied, a chorus of familiar notes which, because they comprised the end and not the beginning of a famous melody, seemed oddly suspended in time. He and the pianist then engaged in a call-and-response of arpeggios, their flurries of notes leading with mathematical logic back to the opening of Duke Ellington's "Sophisticated Lady". When the bassist and drummer joined in, the audience clapped in acknowledgment. Hale's tone was luxuriant, evoking memories of such tenor players of yesteryear as Coleman Hawkins and Don Byas.*

Lee kept writing and flipping the pages of his pad with an intensity that surprised him. After the Quartet played two more songs, Lee looked up to see that the audience was applauding more insistently, and the pianist had risen from his bench to take a small bow. With the set now ending, Lee flipped back the pages to see that he'd filled most of the pad. He heard Hale introduce the bassist and drummer, then all four men left the stage as the applause dwindled. Lee was one of the first to intercept them on their way to the dressing room.

"Great show! Man, I heard and saw some incredible things!"

"Did you get it all down?" Hale asked pointedly.

"Did I?" Lee grinned proudly, then added, "I can't stay for the next set, though. Have to get up for work. But I'll come down again on Sunday."

"That's okay. Bring somebody with you, and I'll tell the owner you're both my guests."

"Thanks," Lee said. "Really." The two men shook hands and parted, the musician rapidly lost in an onslaught of well-wishers and autograph seekers.

Lee turned and made his way out of the club, pushing past the burly doorman who was busy detaining the line of people that clamored to be seated for the already delayed second set. A tall man with shoulder-length, light brown hair and a beard shouted from the queue, "Hey, man, like, how was he playing?"

"It was unreal!"

"Dig it!" The neo-hippie shouted, and Lee got the feeling that the clock had been turned back to 1970 and Hale's music was once again the only constant that mattered on a night like this in this part of the Village. Smiling, he walked away from the And/Or and down a street that now showed no trace of the day's summer rain. Then he laughed out loud and began to run—for no reason at all—down the solitary steps of the subway entrance.

Lee's elation had been usurped by doubt and apathy by the time he turned off the light in his small bedroom. "What's the point? It won't get published," he heard himself say aloud as he pulled a single sheet up over his outstretched body. A normally sound sleeper, he was fitful now, waking once to find his right hand pushing against the wall, another time to see both of his hands gripping the pillow under his face. He noticed there was sweat on his forehead and tried to calm himself. Then he saw it was nearly time for his alarm to buzz anyway, so he threw the pillow to one side of his bed and got up.

The rain came again while he was at work that morning, and by lunchtime it had gotten harder. Lee looked out the window of his cubicle then at his small umbrella and shook his head. He rose from the desk and made his way down the vacant corridor. As an afterthought, he looked for Wendy in her cubicle but she wasn't there. Once he bought his food in the cafeteria, Lee sat down at a table near a window. He ate, watching the storm clouds and the flashes of lightning as he recalled the previous night's event. His thoughts were broken by the sound of a woman's voice.

"Hi, I'm Carmen. Do you mind if I join you?" He detected a slight Spanish accent, looked up and immediately thought that something about her face, with its dark eyes and full lips, was special.

"Sure! My name's Lee," he said, rising halfway out of his seat and gesturing to the one facing him.

"Thanks. You're a junior editor, aren't you?"

"That's right. And you must be new?"

"I started interning with Mr. Gross last week," Carmen offered. "I just graduated from NYU, and working at this magazine seemed like a good way to learn more about the arts scene."

"You're not from New York, then?"

"No, New Mexico," Carmen smiled demurely.

"And are you a musician, or . . ."

"I'm a dancer," she said, then paused to chew her spinach salad. "I've also choreographed some things—that's what I'd like to do, really. Choreography. What else do you do?"

"Me? I'm a writer, I mean, I'd like to get published doing something other than special features for this place."

"What do you write about?" She persisted calmly, not looking up from her plate.

"I just started working on something last night. A piece on a Jazz musician."

"That's cool. I like Jazz . . . and flamenco, mambo, the tango . . . ," Carmen took a sip of her coffee and looked at him, her eyes laughing. But Lee didn't return her gaze because he was staring through the rainy window, lost in thought.

"What are you thinking? Did you not want to talk anymore, Lee?"

Now he looked into her dark eyes and saw genuine concern. "Last night," he began slowly, "I went to see my favorite Jazz musician, Hale Dodge, at a club in the Village. We spoke before the set and he urged me to write about him. He actually let me interview him. Then, when he played, the most wonderful things came into my head. It was like a vision."

"What kind of vision?"

"Oh, you'll laugh," he said, clearing his throat. "He had this tune called 'Rings of Saturn,' and I swear I saw those rings and I even saw the stars in the bell of his horn."

She sipped her coffee again. "Well, I believe music is a magical thing."

"Carmen, do you think this was like a sign, telling me that it's the start of something for me? I mean, I've tried to write about the music before but I've never gotten anywhere, never."

Carmen regarded him for a moment, a thoughtful frown growing on her face. "You should just trust this experience, Lee," she said at last, then brightened. "It's like in dance, when the movements come so naturally it feels like a dream, like you're not even doing it yourself. That's the time you have to trust it. Because, before you know it, something great happens!"

"But what if I write it and no one wants it, it goes nowhere?!" Lee said defiantly, his voice rising.

"If you write it and send it to the right person, someone who loves this music as much as you, . . . then you can't miss," she began with a disarming smile. "What did you say this musician's name was?"

"Hale, Hale Dodge."

"I'd like to hear this Hale Dodge."

"He's playing at the And/Or all this week," Lee said, feeling more hopeful. "Would you like to go hear him with me? He doesn't come to New York much . . ."

"Yes," she interrupted. "Why not?"

"Well, how's Sunday? The sets are early and we can eat dinner there. I'll also get a chance to talk to him again."

"That's good. Will I meet him, too?"

"Sure, why not?" Lee grinned.

"You must call me," Carmen said, writing her name and home telephone number on a napkin and passing it to him.

"I meant to ask, ah, did your parents like opera?"

"No," Carmen laughed. "That name's been in the Rojas family for ages—long before Bizet."

"It's a nice name," Lee said softly.

Not wanting to betray the eagerness in his heart, Lee merely waved and smiled whenever he saw Carmen in the office the next day then waited until that evening to call her. They made arrangements to meet at the club before the first set on Sunday. Lee proposed staying for both sets and, to his surprise, she readily agreed.

The rainstorms of the first half of the week gave way to a hot, dry spell, and Sunday evening bore a temperature above 80 degrees. When Lee reached the top of the subway station steps this time, he immediately saw Carmen standing beside the entrance of the And/Or, waiting. She seemed even prettier than at work: her face was calmer, her dancer's figure seemed more elegant in a short, royal blue, sleeveless dress. She failed to see him approach until he was just a few yards away. As he greeted her with an embrace, she kissed him quickly on the cheek.

"Don't worry, I'm not wearing lipstick," she smiled.

"Not worried at all, just glad to see you," Lee said and took her hand as they moved toward the Jazz club's entrance.

After they were seated at a table, Lee asked her, "Does anything on the menu grab you?"

165

"I hope not!"

Lee laughed until he heard a familiar voice over his shoulder. "Glad you came back, Mr. Sanford. And who's your charming guest?"

"Hale!" Lee said, whirling around in his chair. "Meet Carmen Rojas." Carmen rose and they shook hands.

"Did you have more questions or are you straight?" Hale leaned forward and asked Lee in a hushed tone.

"Well, there is something. Will you excuse me, Carmen?" When she nodded, Lee went to the bar with the musician.

"That's a nice lady there, man. *Muy bonita.* Does she dig the music, too?"

"Thanks. Yeah, she does," Lee murmured, folding his hands on the bar. "Hale, I'm almost embarrassed to tell you this . . ."

"Is it about what you felt or saw when I was playing the other night?"

"How'd you know?"

"You're not the first it's happened to, nor will you be the last," the musician replied, his voice unusually vibrant. "This has been going on for thousands of years, probably since the dawn of music. It's happened to me, listening to musicians who were really spiritually advanced, who, as the Native Americans say, 'have strong medicine'. It usually happens *to* people who are spiritually open, listening to music that's spiritually giving, and listening in-person so the message comes face-to-face. Happened to me a number of times, man. And there are times I've helped to give the experience, the messages, to others."

"But what does it mean?"

"The message you received?" When Lee nodded, Hale continued. "For you, it's about liberation. It's what you need right now so you won't be afraid. The music sent you a message, not just me. That's the magic. There's no drugs or tricks here, just spirits and universal consciousness: the wider world. Without liberation, you can't experience the wider world, man. Liberation is the thing this so-called 'Free Jazz' is all about when it's done right, and not 'liberation armies' and people dying in the streets. It's liberating the mind and the soul. It's my mission. And now you've got it, too. So trust it, grow with it. You can't lose it unless you foolishly *try* to lose it." Hale then abruptly left him at the bar and went to join the rest of the Quartet on the bandstand. Lee looked around the room, surprised to see that all of the tables of the And/Or were now full, and people were still coming through the door. He made his way back to Carmen and sat down.

"Sorry I took so long."

"It's okay, Lee," she reassured him with a wave of her hand. "I just ordered myself a glass of wine. You two had a heavy conversation going, huh?"

"Well, remember I told you how last time, all these ideas and images came to me?" He leaned across the table to be heard above the chatter of the other customers. She nodded, and he continued. "It really was like having a vision, and Hale confirmed that's what it was . . . it's happened to him, too. And other people have told him they've had the same experience listening to his music."

"That's serious. I believe it," Carmen responded. As the people around them began to hush attentively, they both turned to look at the musicians. A waitress appeared at one side of the table, and they whispered their dinner orders to her hurriedly. The lights dimmed, there was an announcement and applause, and then silence. Hale brought the soprano sax to his lips and the group began to play Thelonious Monk's "'Round Midnight" as a slow tango. She turned to Lee, her eyes gleaming in disbelief. "What a coincidence! The last piece I choreographed at NYU, I used this same rhythm."

"Maybe, he knows," Lee answered softly and smiled.

Lee found himself watching Carmen as much as he watched the band. Sometimes he marveled at the strong, graceful lines of her neck when she leaned back to see one of the musicians better. Other times he watched how the light from the small candle on their table combined with the blueness of her dress to bring out orange undertones in the beige skin of her long, smooth arms. As much as desire, he felt a strange yet appealing comfort just being with her.

"Did you really enjoy it?" He asked Carmen when the applause for the first set ended and the musicians left the stage.

"They're really good," she replied emphatically. "I didn't see the . . . images, but I really felt something, something very positive."

"That's good enough."

Carmen smiled and began to rise. "Excuse me while I freshen up."

Lee smiled back then watched her go. "Do you want to see the dessert list?" The waitress's voice abruptly refocused his attention.

"No. But we'd both like more white wine, thanks."

When Carmen returned to their table, the dinner plates had been cleared, new wine had arrived, and the musicians had returned to the bandstand area. "What a line outside the Ladies'," she said, still flabbergasted. "I thought I would miss the start of the music."

"Don't worry," he smiled. "The musicians just came back early to chat with their fans. This is their last night in town, you know."

"Oh, right. That gives us a little while to talk, then."

"Yeah, tell me more about the piece you choreographed. The tango?"

"Let me tell you," Carmen began animatedly, her descriptions of the dancers' movements lasting until the dimming of the lights for the start of the second and last set.

"This first tune is a new one," Hale intoned over the customers' dying chatter. "It's something I wrote this week for a very talented friend of mine. I call it, 'The Scribe'."

When the musician glanced at Lee before putting the tenor sax to his lips, Carmen stared from one man to the other with her mouth gaping in amazement. Lee raised his eyebrows at her. Then he reached into his jacket for his pad and pen. "Okay?" He whispered. She made the "ok" sign with her fingers, then watched him as he wrote.

The meditative song ended to loud applause, and Hale introduced the next one as "Quest in the Mirror". After the band played the mysterious-sounding melody in free time, Lee stopped writing to regard Carmen. She was looking at him intently, her mouth open slightly as if she wanted to speak but something kept her from doing so. Hale's tenor sax soloed tenderly, and the band settled into waltz time. Lee looked into her eyes but remained engrossed in the music at the same time. As Hale's solo gave way to the bassist's bowed solo, Lee saw a mirror with Carmen on one side and he on the other. Both of them studied the glass, searching for something in their respective views. Then they reached out simultaneously, the mirror disappeared, and their hands joined, then their bodies became one. When the song ended, Lee found that he was still looking at Carmen. He reached for her hand while the audience clapped. "Did you hear it? Could you see it? It was like I could see us together, finding each other, in a mirror!"

"Yes," she answered, and waited for the applause to fade before continuing. "It seemed like this search, this quest in the mirror was for someone like you . . . someone to love." She blushed, tightened her grip on his hand, and added, "Lee, I'm . . . this is scary."

"I know." He grasped her hand more firmly, and they looked at each other in silent affirmation.

""'Levitation' will be the last song for this set, and this week," Hale said slowly as the drummer used his brushes to play an uptempo calypso beat behind him.

"I think this song is for us, too," Lee grinned.

"Why? Do you feel levitated?"

"Positively levitated!"

Carmen let go of his hand and laughed, enjoying his pleasure. The bassist, who had been watching the couple, leaned over to the pianist and said, "Just look at those two, they're swingin'!"

The drummer deftly switched to his sticks, playing louder, and then the pianist and bassist joined him. Hale came back to the microphone with a bass clarinet in his hand. He started with a simple, lilting melody then dove into a high-spirited solo. As the drummer's accents syncopated the beat, the crowd began to applaud in time to the basic rhythm. Hale danced, bobbing and weaving, blowing his horn the whole time. He also turned sideways, his bass clarinet's bell still near the mike, and then he turned again and strutted backwards off the bandstand. He stood there for a moment, whooping and howling over the driving calypso beat through his horn. Then he bowed down abruptly, honking from a crouching position. The rhythmic clapping turned into wild applause and cheers, and Hale ended his solo with a series of softer and softer, rhythmic squeaks. He slowly rose to more cheering, his saxophone and flute cases slung over each arm and the bass clarinet in one hand. The rest of the Quartet continued to play and some of the customers, including Lee and Carmen, clapped to the drummer's beat again. Hale nodded once to the crowd, turned and left the bandstand, half-dancing down the aisle leading to the musicians' dressing rooms and the back door of the club.

The pianist took a rollicking solo, receiving cheers and whistles when he quoted Sonny Rollins' classic, "St. Thomas". After an appropriately polyrhythmic drum solo and more cheering, the pianist led the band back to the melody and closed out the song. While applause and pleasant chatter reigned, Lee's face was frought with concern. He rose and approached the bandstand with Carmen following. "Where's Hale?" He asked the pianist.

"I don't know," the pianist replied. "The owner told me

he doesn't know either but Hale left us our money. I know I'm paid!"

"Baby, you never can tell with Hale," the drummer chimed in while breaking down his kit. "But I still love him."

"How odd," Lee said absently, and stepped off the bandstand. "I wanted to talk to him."

"We should be going now," Carmen urged gently, taking Lee by the arm.

After leaving the And/Or, the couple walked hand-in-hand several paces and stopped. "I don't know why he left so suddenly," Lee sighed and shook his head. "But he is a man of mysterious comings and goings."

"I enjoyed myself very much, Lee." He looked into her eyes then, unconsciously, at her lips. They moved toward each other and kissed.

"This is wonderful," he sighed, holding her close. "When can I see you again?"

"The day after tomorrow. Tomorrow I go to the dance studio."

"Let's meet outside the club again. There's a place I know around the corner, we can eat there. The food's better than the And/Or's."

"Good. I didn't like theirs much either," Carmen replied, scrunching her nose up then giggling. Lee rested his right hand on the small of her back. She looked at him and they kissed deeply.

"You have to go now, I know," Lee almost whispered in her ear as they hugged. Standing there together, with her long, black hair against his cheek, he closed his eyes and got the feeling time was standing still.

"Yes, I do," she answered after awhile. "But I'll see you at work tomorrow." She stepped back and they looked into each others' eyes while holding hands. Carmen slowly let go and turned to face the street. She hailed a taxicab. When it stopped, Lee helped her into it, they kissed goodbye, and he strode happily up the block to the subway station.

The next day, Lee's usual late Monday afternoon reverie was broken by a hand on his shoulder. "I picked up the paper when I went out for lunch. You must read this," Carmen said ominously.

His smile of greeting turned into a puzzled stare as he took the paper from her. He scanned the page until he was struck by the headline: "Jazzman Dodge Missing, Believed Dead". Underneath, in smaller type, it read: "Hotel Room Abandoned After Leaving Nightclub". He hurriedly read the short article then looked at Carmen. "This can't be! I mean, it's like him to disappear and then reappear halfway across the globe in a few weeks."

"Maybe you should send what you're writing to the guy who wrote this," she suggested, sitting down next to him. "You reviewed his last . . . his latest performance, and if this guy cares about Hale like you do . . . ."

"I will, Carmen. That's a great idea. I just can't believe he's dead." Lee opened his desk drawer and began to leaf through the pad he had taken to the club.

"See you tomorrow?"

"Yes, Seven-thirty," he said, and kissed Carmen before she rose to leave.

That evening, Lee stayed up past midnight turning his review and interview into an article built around the contention that Hale Dodge was a spiritually-inclined and unconventional musician who was playing better than ever, had much to live for, and had probably just left the scene for now. The newspaper writer he sent it to turned out to be a senior entertainment editor who liked it and had it published. Lee and Carmen continued to see each other and, one day in early autumn, they confessed their love for each other. The week they became engaged, that same senior editor called Lee to tell him to contact a friend of his who edited *The Jam*, a national Jazz magazine. Lee impressed the editor, and took a new job as a *Jam* staff writer covering the New York/New Jersey club and concert scene. Weeks later, Carmen left their style magazine, too, after auditioning for and landing a placement with a local dance company. The following April, Lee and Carmen were married and they found a small apartment in the Village.

At the start of the summer, Lee received an assignment from *The Jam* to interview an elderly trumpeter who had been coaxed out of semi-retirement after the musician's long out-of-print recordings had been re-issued on CD to widespread acclaim. Since the trumpeter now lived in Brooklyn, Lee took the subway to one of the Prospect Park stops, deciding to take advantage of the sunny weather by walking through the Park to the interview.

"I haven't been here in years," Lee mused to himself as he saw the familiar sights of dogs being walked by joggers and West Indian nannies doting on their young charges. He found himself listening to birds singing in the trees as he ambled along one of the asphalt paths. Walking further, he soon detected another song—a song played on a flute. He stopped to listen, and bicyclists raced past him as the memories crowded each other in his mind. He sprinted down the path as fast as he could and followed the sound until he reached a clearing. He looked around, scanning the grassy field now before him. He stepped into the field and listened. The flute song was louder and clearer, and he looked up to see a familiar bend of tall trees on the crest of the hill on the opposite side of the field. Then the flute song stopped.

"Hale?!" He called loudly, his hands raised to his mouth.

After a pause, he heard the faintest sound of grass being crunched underfoot. Then a familiar figure emerged from the bend of trees with a canvas bag over his shoulder and a wooden flute in one hand. He stepped sideways down the sloping field, moving faster as he approached Lee.

"Hey, Sanford! Something told me I'd see you here today."

APPENDIX I

COMPOSERS' CREDITS

In alphabetical order, the following composers must be credited for writing music to which I wrote lyrics which have been published for the first time in this volume. The composers' publishing companies are noted in parentheses.

John Coltrane—"Olé" (Jowcol Music/BMI)
Duke Ellington & Billy Strayhorn—"The Single Petal Of A Rose" (Tempo Music Inc./ASCAP)
Bobby Hutcherson—"Tranquility" (Blue Horizon Music/BMI)
Thelonious Monk—"Ask Me Now" (Thelonious Music/BMI)
Herbie Nichols—"2300 Skiddoo" (Northern Music Co./ASCAP)
Mal Waldron—"The Seagulls of Kristiansund" (Enja/GEMA)

APPENDIX II

PUBLICATION NOTES

None of the poems or lyrics in this volume have been previously published in print form with the exception of "Poem for Gil Evans," which appeared in the June 1988 edition (Vol. 1V, No. 10) of the WKCR-FM *Program Guide* and is reprinted here by permission.

The following poems and lyrics were first presented to the public in "live" performance by the author with his Jazz & Poetry ensemble, "Elliot Bratton's Message," or with other groups he performed with, during the years 1985-1991: "A Lunar Desire," "A Meditation of Hope," "Blue Psalm," "The Burning Men of Harlem," "Early Summer Nights," "The Hope In You," "Human Unity," "I've Never Been Rested," "Lady, Come Sing To Me," "Move the Blood," "The Prophet Disappeared," "The Shadow of Human Fate," "Taylorreality," "There Is A Time For Truth," and "You Got The Blues".

In addition, the author also read his poetry during certain broadcasts on WKCR-FM during the years 1983-90, sometimes adding music in the background. (For example,

"The Clocks Strike Twelve," was read for Halloween to Mal Waldron's solo piano performance of his suitably eerie "Here, There and Everywhere".) These poems were first presented by the author on WKCR: "A Fickle Sonance," "A Poem for Rahsaan," "The Clocks Strike Twelve," "For Blackwell," "Half-Mast," "Monk's Mood," "Near-Yet-Far," "Neither Is Jazz," "Prayer for the Silence," "Rhymes For Our Times," and "Supreme, As Night".

BVG